JOB SEARCH AND STOP PROCRASTINATION

2-in-1 Book

The New Approach to Boost Your Career Hunting (including Tips for Job Interview) + Simple Yet Effective Strategies to Become Highly Productive

Job Search: Using Technology To Get The Right Job

The New Approach to Boost Your Career Hunting (including Tips for Job Interview) + Simple Yet Effective Strategies to Become Highly Productive

Table of Contents

INTRODUCTION.. 6

Chapter 1 - The Hunt Begins 10

   Seven Simple Ways to Find the Job You Love. 11

   Using the Internet to Find Your Dream Job 16

   How to Find Jobs that Aren't Advertised. 18

Chapter 2—A Resume to Beat Them All 22

   Creating a Killer Resume. 22

   How to Tailor Your Resume to a Specific Job. 27

   How to Write Great Cover Letters. 30

Chapter 3 - Get Ahead with an Online Portfolio 37

   The Lowdown on Creating an Irresistible LinkedIn Profile. 41

   How a Blog Can Boost Your Career. 46

   Six Fabulous Tools to Help You Put Together Your Online Portfolio. 48

Chapter 5—Shameless Self-Promotion 61

Chapter 6—Breaking Barriers 73

Chapter 7—Job Interview Secrets 87

Chapter 8—Make It Happen 98

Conclusion 107

INTRODUCTION

Finding the job that is right for you can be a difficult, complicated, and sometimes stressful process. Whether you are looking for your first job, a better job, or a career change job, you'll need to develop a plan on how to do so and then you'll need to find out the best ways to get that job you're looking for. Many people have job or career aspirations, but they get stuck at where they're at because they don't have a clue on how to get that job or career.

In this book, I'm going to provide you with the tools and tips you'll need to get the job you want. I'll tell you how you can find those jobs, whether they are advertised or not. I will also tell you how to position yourself above other candidates who are applying for the same job.

My name is David Allen. I am a how-to-get-a-job expert. I've had years of experience as a human resource director for multiple companies in different industries. I have also worked as a recruiter, recruiting people to fill various corporate job openings. And, finally, I have worked as a job consultant, helping people find their optimum jobs. Over the years, I have accumulated a lot of knowledge regarding the best way for people to get the jobs in which they're interested. In my experiences, I've found that many people do not know how to go about getting their dream job and, as a result, they never knew that an opening for that job existed, or they didn't know how to place themselves in a position to get the job they would have loved to have had. People I have worked with in my human resources, recruiting and counseling positions have often encouraged me to write a book and share my vast knowledge and years of experience with others who could benefit from it. With that in mind, I've written this book.

If you'll just take the time to read this book, and if you'll use the tips and suggestions which apply to your particular situation, you'll have a great chance to get the job you want. Through the years, I have helped people get jobs or careers they never thought they'd have a chance to get. Depending on the career you are interested in and the level you are at with your own job experiences, each career or job requires a different approach. There is not one single way to find the job you want. Cookie-cutter approaches and job-hunting templates don't work, as each industry, each job, each employer is different. That's why I intend to give you a number of ways to find and get the dream job you are looking for. After reading this book, you will also find that you'll be more efficient in your job search. You'll learn where to look for jobs, how to look for jobs, and then to go after the jobs you're interested in. Not only will this information save you time, it will also give you a better chance to secure the job in which you're interested and place you above the clutter of applicants for the same position.

As a career counselor, I have been able to help many people find jobs or careers that suit them. Whether they were looking to make more money, utilize their talents, or find a work environment or career that better suited them, I've been able to point them in the right direction and counsel them on how they might go about achieving success as they search for the job or career of their choice. I've received thanks from people who maintain that the help I provided was life-altering. I am hoping that I can do the same with you and, maybe one day, I will receive a testimonial from you telling me that you are forever grateful on how the tips in this book placed you on the right career path.

If you'll read this short book and if you'll implement the tips and techniques which apply to you, I can assure you that you'll have a chance to be your best self in finding the job you want. In my younger days, an old coffee buddy of mine and I would often talk about the dream jobs we wanted to have one day. Early on in our discussions, we determined something that still applies today: You will never be able to get that dream job if you don't apply for it. So, the moral of the story with job hunting is simple: You are very unlikely to get a job that you don't pursue. As an aside to that, how you pursue that job may well determine whether you get the job or not. If you read this book and follow the tips which are appropriate for you, you'll have the best chance of getting that job. No, I can't guarantee that you'll get any job you apply for, but I'll guarantee that you will have your best chance in getting that job.

I have a friend of mine who has written many self-help books and he is considered an expert in that field. He tells me that there are two kinds of people that will read self-help books such as this one. There are those that will read the books and place the tips and techniques on a backburner, often never getting back to them. Then there are those who read the books and implement immediately the tips and techniques they derive from the book. I'm sure you can guess which of the two types of readers are more successful. Hopefully, you'll find yourself in the group that implements the knowledge you gain immediately. This will give you the best chance of succeeding in your efforts to secure a new job.

The tips and techniques I'm providing in this book can provide incredible results, if you take the time and make the effort to implement them. Every chapter in this book is full of information on how you can go about getting the job you want. Let's get after it…together we can make it happen.

Chapter 1 - The Hunt Begins

Where do I start, you ask. Looking for a job can seem overwhelming, especially at the beginning of your search. This is why it will be important for you to develop a plan before you begin to apply for specific jobs or at specific companies. Here are some steps you can follow in preparing to find the job you really want.

Decide What You Want. There are tons of job openings out there for prospective employees to choose from. Before you place yourself into all this clutter, you should first ask yourself some questions that will help you define and refine the jobs you want to look for. What kind of job to you want to look for? (A marketing job, a sales job, a customer service job, etc.) Chances are that you'll already have a good idea as to what kind of job you are looking for. If not, I suggest that you get on some of the online job sites such as LinkedIn, Indeed, or Glassdoor, and browse the different categories to determine which type of jobs might appeal to you.

Also, you should determine what type of company you would like to work for. A large company, a small company, a medium-sized company or maybe it doesn't matter to you. Are you concerned with having a good working environment. If so, do any companies you're interested in have solid reputations for the working environment they provide? Have you had any previous experience which might be helpful to you in securing a job in any certain industry or company.

Job Search

As an example, the son of a friend of mine worked as a public relations person for a franchised restaurant chain. This was his first job out of college. He loved the restaurant industry, but he wanted to move from a public relations job to a marketing job. As a result, he decided to target restaurant chains (small and large) and franchised businesses (not just restaurants, but other franchised operations). This young man knew that his experience in restaurants and his experience with a franchised company could separate him from other applicants who did not have the same experience. So, in looking for a new job, it will be helpful to determine what previous experience you've had that might help you rise above other people who are applying for the same jobs.

Once you have determined the types of jobs you want and the types of companies you would like to work for, you'll want to develop a resume. In the next chapter of this book, I will outline specifically how you can develop a "killer" resume, however, before we do that, I'd like to give you some quick ideas on how you'll be using that resume.

Seven Simple Ways to Find the Job You Love.

1) **Social networks.** If you already have a presence on social media platforms such as Facebook, Twitter, and LinkedIn, those platforms can provide an excellent means for you to get the word out that you are looking for a job. The exception to that, of course, is if you already have a job and you want to keep it quiet that you are looking for another job. In that case, you won't want to use social networks to inform people that you are looking for a job. But if you are currently not employed or if you have a job and your current employer knows you are looking for another job, then social networks will provide a

great way for you to get the word out. My thought on looking for jobs is that the person looking for the job should "Tell the World". I advise people to let as many people as possible know that you are looking for a job, as you never know who will be able to help you with that.

2) If you don't already have a Facebook or Twitter presence, then I doubt that establishing a presence on those platforms is going to help you with this job search. On the other hand, I strongly recommend that you establish a LinkedIn presence even if you don't have one now, as this could produce immediate results, possibly or probably from someone you don't even know now.

3) **Target companies directly.** Are there any companies in particular that you would really like to work for? Any companies that you think would be a great fit for you? If so, I suggest that you target those companies directly. You can do this in a number of different ways. The best way is probably to get on the company's web site. Many companies who have a web site, especially the larger companies, will feature job opportunities on their site. Often these job opportunities are posted on a page which you can access on a tab that is often labeled jobs or job opportunities, careers or career opportunities, or employment. These pages will allow you to determine if there are any current openings and what those openings are. If there are no openings in the field you're looking for and if you are really interested, I'd advise you not to get discouraged. Just because there are no openings today doesn't mean that there won't be an opening soon. If you really like the idea of working for this company, you might still send them a cover letter and resume, detailing specifically why you want to work for that company or why you think you would be a good fit. In these instances, I suggest that you specifically get the name of the person who would be responsible for

hiring. For example, if you are interested in a marketing position, you should call the company and get the name, the proper title, and the correct spelling of the person who is in charge of the company's marketing department. Yes, you could do this in an email, but emails are very easy to delete and forget, so I would recommend that you use an old-fashioned letter sent through the US Post Office. Obviously, you won't want to do this for every company you apply to, however I encourage you to send to any specific companies in which you have interest and, if they don't have any current openings, ask them to keep on file for future reference whenever they have openings. I also found that something that is written or printed on paper is much more difficult to discard than an email which can be deleted with the simple click of a button.

And one other thing with these targeted letters and resumes. Unless their web site directs you otherwise, I would suggest that you send the letters to the person who will actually be in charge of the hiring. i.e.— For a marketing job, your letter would be better directed at the Vice President or Director of Marketing than it would be to the Human Resources Director. (Also, please note that there would be no harm in sending letters to both.)

4) **Use your school as a resource.** If you have any kind of post high school degree, whether it is a college degree, a technical or community college degree, a vocational or trade degree, you should know that those schools are very likely to have departments which can assist alumni in getting jobs. As most educational institutions like to frame their reputations on the jobs that their graduates get, they can be very helpful in referring alumni to job openings. By the same token, employers often use these school career centers to post job openings. A friend of mine who owns a small business has

repeatedly hired employees from a nearby vocational school, as he knows that these employees are well-trained and also because he doesn't have to pay to advertise the job openings. And he also likes the fact that he will not be flooded with applications from people who have not had the proper training or who haven't refined their job search. For years, I have hired summer interns by contacting the nearby college and I have always been impressed with the selection of candidates they provide me with. So, whether you are looking for you first job after graduating from one of these post high school institutions or whether you have already had other jobs since your graduation, you should certainly consider them as a possible resource in finding your next job.

5) **Job fairs/career fairs**. Many colleges and universities, many communities and towns have job fairs in which employers have booths in which you can talk with representatives regarding job openings and opportunities. As someone who is looking for a job, these job fairs offer you the opportunity to meet with multiple employers, almost all of whom are hiring, and to find out what opportunities they might have available. They should be able to tell you what jobs there are specifically available and they will also be able to tell you how you might go about applying for a job there. If you are going to attend only of these job fairs, I suggest that you bring a supply of resumes that you can leave with any employers who you have interest in.

6) **Get the word out...to everyone.** This goes back to my "Tell the World" approach. If you're looking for a new job, I think it's important for you to tell as many people as possible about your interest in finding a new job. Again, you can never be sure who you might get an important referral from or an

important parcel of information that will be helpful to you in getting the job you want. I know a woman who got important information about a job opening from the barista at her coffee shop. I know a man who got his foot in the door for his dream job by mentioning the fact that he wanted to get into a particular company at a birthday party for his niece. One of the in-laws there was a golfing buddy of one of the higher-ups in the company and, through this connection, the man who was looking for a job got an interview that he never would have been able to secure otherwise. Book clubs, parties, happy hours, volunteer activities—these all offer chances for you to spread the news that you are looking for a job.

Again, it should be pointed out that if you have a current job, you will probably have to be somewhat discreet in spreading the word that you are looking for another job, as you may not want that information to impact your current work situation.

7) **Professional organizations, associations.** You should also know that professional organizations or associations can be excellent sources for job openings in your particular field. Regardless of what profession or field you are in, there is probably an organization for the members of that profession.

A friend of mine secured his first job as a newspaper reporter through the Society of Professional Journalists. He contacted the local chapter president and that president was able to put him in contact with a newspaper that was looking to fill a reporter position. Another friend of mine has a son who recently graduated from vocational school in which he earned an electrician's degree. That man got his job by contacting the local electrician's union. They were able to refer him to two different employers that were hiring electricians.

8) **"Now Hiring" posters/"Help Wanted" signs.** As I write this book, the economy in the U.S. is very strong and there are many job openings. When the economy is strong like this, you'll note that many, many businesses have "Now Hiring" or "Help Wanted" signs posted on their premises. If you think that any of these businesses would be a good place to work, I suggest that you visit the location and ask to speak to the manager or to complete an application. Are there any businesses you frequent that seem like they would be great places to work? If so, you may want to ask who does the hiring there and then introduce yourself. It should be noted that this is a great way to get seasonal jobs if you are looking to make extra cash. (i.e.-The holiday season.)

Using the Internet to Find Your Dream Job

It shouldn't surprise you to find out that the internet provides a great way to help you find and get your dream job. On the other hand, internet information is so readily available and the fact that a person can complete a job application in the comfort of his own living room (maybe even wearing pajamas), often leads to many more applications for the same job. Here are some ways you can use the internet to get your dream job:

1) **Monitor job openings directly on a company's web site.** I detailed this in the previous section. A company's web site often offers a great way to find out if they have any current openings.

2) **Research your desired company.** In the "old days", people who were interested to work for a specific company were encouraged to get their hands on the company's annual report or the company's promotional literature. This information would hopefully provide enough information about the company so that the job applicant could refer to some of this information in his cover letter. Now, it is extremely easy to learn about any company you might be interested. You can simply go to their web site, where you can get lots of information about the products they sell or the services they offer. If you're smart, you'll use some of the information you glean from the web site in your cover letter to the company (along with your resume, of course.)

3) **Find great companies to work for.** There's no lack of "great companies to work for" information on the internet. If you are not totally sure of what company you want to work for, but you know that you just want to work for a good company, the internet is full of articles on which companies are great to work for. If you have a particular area or region in mind, you can easily fine-tune your search. i.e.-Great companies to work for in Boston area.

4) **Professional associations, organizations.** Again, I covered some of this in the previous section, but the internet provides a great way for you to find out the names and contact information of professional organizations, associations, unions, fraternities, etc. Many of these organizations post their newsletters online or allow you to get free emailed copies of their newsletter. Newsletters provide another great way for you to learn about the industry you are interested in. Some of them even contain job postings.

5) **Job sites.** There are many job search sites on the internet. Many employers use these sites to post job openings and secure applications. If you're looking for a job, it is important to remember that many companies use only one or two sites to post their job openings and just because you don't find an opening for a company on one site doesn't mean that it will not be posted on another site. I suggest that you start out by browsing multiple job sites and then as you become more familiar with the sites, you'll be able to determine which sites you feel most comfortable with, which sites offer the most jobs in your field, etc.

Some of the most popular job sites currently include: Indeed, Monster, Glassdoor, ZipRecruiter, and CareerBuilder. I encourage you to browse each of these sites a number of times and then if you want to eliminate some of them from you rostrum, you can do so after you determine which ones are most likely to be effective for your search.

How to Find Jobs that Aren't Advertised.

Nearly half of all available job openings are never advertised, so you'll need to keep this in mind as you do your search. Some companies don't advertise job openings because of the cost involved. Others don't advertise because they're interested to hire from within. And some companies don't want to advertise because they don't want to sort through the multitude of applications they might receive through advertising an opening.

Job Search

Its important to note that nearly half of all jobs are not advertised. As someone who is looking for a job, this means that you'll have to find ways to access these unadvertised jobs.

The most popular means of finding unadvertised jobs is through some sort of networking. Social networks such as Facebook and Twitter can be effective in helping you find these jobs. In order to do that however, you'll probably need to have an established presence on these sites. Someone who has 750 to 1000 Facebook or Twitter followers is certainly likely to be more successful than someone who has a couple dozen followers. And if you have a limited number of followers on your social media platforms, it's going to be difficult for you to gain a larger number of followers in a short time. So, if you have a solid presence on Facebook or Twitter, I'd suggest that you consider them as a possible source for information or referrals in your job search.

Even if you don't have much of a presence on Facebook or Twitter, I strongly suggest that you establish a presence on LinkedIn, which is primarily a business site that has groups for specific industries. For example, if you are an engineer, LinkedIn has a group specifically for engineers. If you are a marketeer, LinkedIn has specific groups for marketing professionals. These groups include not only people looking for jobs, but employers who are looking to hire people and recruiters who are looking to place people.

Another benefit to LinkedIn is that it offers you the opportunity to apply for multiple jobs in just a short amount of time. You'll save time by not having to write cover letters. You'll also save time by not having to fill out some of the tedious applications which are required on some of the job search or individual company sites. As a matter of fact, you might be able to apply for up to 20 jobs in just 30 minutes.

Job Search

(It might take you 30 minutes to apply for just one job on an individual company site or one of the internet job search sites.) Depending on what kind of job you're looking for, you should remember that looking for jobs can sometimes be a numbers game. The more jobs you apply for, the better chance you have of getting a job. LinkedIn is a great medium for this approach and I encourage you to use it as such.

And, as discussed before, don't ignore other possible sources for unadvertised job openings. This includes alumni associations or school career centers and professional associations or organizations. And if you have established a target company or companies, don't hesitate to contact them even if they are not advertising any openings. A company that has no openings today may be only a day away from having an opening…or, even better, they may have an opening that they haven't advertised yet.

One other piece of advice as you begin your job hunt. Try not to focus on the rejections or the non-responses that you receive. As mentioned above, job hunting is often a numbers game and you're more likely to get an interview or a job by applying for many jobs than you are if you apply for just a few jobs. I had a friend who, when he looked for a job, would send out one resume at a time, waiting to receive a response from that application before he sent out another application. When he finally admitted that his process didn't make sense, he sent out multiple applications at the same time, realizing that he could never control whether a prospective employer was interested in him or not. My friend finally realized that it only takes one yes to make up for all the rejections and non-responses. He realized that he couldn't control the results, but he could control the process. He resolved to apply for at least 10 jobs per day until he had an acceptable job offer. It ends up that he had three invitations to interview within a week. And he finally had to choose between two attractive offers. That was a nice problem to have and he admitted later that once he had discovered the process he needed to use to get a job, the results followed…quickly.

Chapter 2—A Resume to Beat Them All

Creating a Killer Resume.

If you're going to have a chance to get your dream job, your first goal should be to get your "foot in the door". If you can't get an interview, you won't have a chance to get the job you want. A top-notch resume will be an extremely important tool for you to use in securing interviews.

In developing a resume, it's important to remember that the company or person you're sending your resume to will most likely be receiving lots of applications for the same job and, in order for you to have a chance, your resume will have to make you stand out among other applicants.

With this in mind, here are some simple steps you can use to create a killer resume:

1) **Review resume samples.** Before you establish your own resume, it will be beneficial for you to know what other resumes look like. You'll find resume samples all over the internet, including resume samples that are categorized according to specific professions, such as advertising, marketing, sales, accounting, nursing, secretarial,

janitorial…just about any profession you can imagine. When you review these resume samples, you should place yourself in the shoes of the person who is doing the hiring and decide which resume formats would appeal to you if you were in the hiring position. And please note that resumes are often catered to specific professions. For example, a resume for an advertising position is likely to be set up differently than a resume for an accounting position. Once you have a feel for what kind of resume you want to develop, you should…

2) **Find a resume template.** A template provides a cookie-cutter approach for you to use in developing your resume. It provides a starting point for you to use in setting up your resume. Although you will most likely be modifying or tweaking your resume for each job you apply for, the resume template will provide you with a structure to use in making sure that you have included all pertinent information on the resume. There are tons of different free resume templates on the internet, including some different options from Microsoft Word. I suggest that you review some different templates and find one that fits your personality and also the type of job for which you are applying. Again, the profession you are applying for may determine how creative you will want to be with your resume design. For example, a person who is applying for an advertising or graphic arts position may well be expected to have a more visually appealing resume than a person who is applying for an accounting or a janitorial position. If you're looking for an internet site that shows a nice variety of sample resumes for specific professions, I suggest myperfectresume.com, where they have resume examples for lots of different professions, ranging from social services to transportation to restaurant and hotel hospitality to retail to information technology…just about any professional

category you can imagine. This site also offers some free templates for you to use in developing your resume.

3) **Determine a font.** After you've determined the template you're going to use for your resume, you should determine a font to use for the resume. For those of you who are not familiar with what a font is, it is simply the typestyle you will use for the words in your resume. If you are typing your resume in a Microsoft Word document, you will be able to choose what font you want to use. In determining a font for your resume, again please keep the person who is doing the hiring in mind. I always suggest that people use simple, basic fonts for their resumes, making the resume as easy to read as possible. You won't want to use a fancy typestyle on your resume; that's not an effective way to stand out among other applicants.

4) **Add your contact information.** Obviously, you'll want to list all of your contact information on your resume, including your phone number(s), your email address, and at least the city and state where you live. Some applicants will choose to list their entire address; others do not. Either way, the goal is for the company or person doing the hiring to be able to contact you easily. If you have multiple phone numbers, I suggest that you give them the number that you will answer all the time. The same goes for email addresses. If you have multiple email addresses, you need to make sure that you give them you should give them only your preferred email address. And then make sure you are checking your phone and email messages daily. I had a young man I was mentoring who did not check his email messages every day and, as a result, he missed an invitation to interview for a job he had applied for.

Job Search

If you're applying for jobs, it's important that you are accessible for prospective employers.

5) **Write your objective.** At or near the top of every resume, you should write your objective in applying for the job. This is a part of a resume which is often customized, based on the specifics of the job you're applying for. With one or two sentences, you'll list why you are applying for the position. For example, a young woman who was applying for a restaurant chain marketing position listed her objectives as follows: "I am looking to meld my three years of marketing experience with my two years of working for a franchised printing chain in a hospitality-oriented industry." As another example, a man looking for a job as a bookseller with Barnes & Noble listed his career objectives as follows: "I have been a loyal and frequent Barnes & Noble customer for years. As an avid reader, I am knowledgeable in many book genres, and I am interested to use my passion for and my knowledge of books into a career as a bookseller." With your objective, you will be telling the hirer why you are applying for the position and also, hopefully, why you are a good fit to be hired for that position.

6) **List important and relevant accomplishments.** With any resume, it will be important for you to list any information that will be relevant to the job you are applying for. This information should be placed in order of relevance to the open position. Again, referring back to the young woman who was applying for a chain restaurant marketing position, the fact that she had three years marketing experience was obviously relevant to the position she was applying for. Along the same lines, since that restaurant chain was a chain that had multiple

franchised locations, she mentioned that she had experience working with a franchised chain. Even though her experience was with a franchised print shop chain instead of a restaurant chain, she realized that her experience in working with franchisees of any sort might well be beneficial or applicable to in the position she was applying for.

7) **Pay attention to the job description and use keywords from this description in your resume.** There are a couple of reasons why you need to refer to keywords in the job description for any job you are applying for. First, you may or may not be aware that some companies use software bots or software programs to pre-screen applications. These bots or software programs are designed to search for keywords that apply to the open job position. These bots are used to filter out resumes that may not pertain specifically to the job opening that was advertised. Some companies are inundated with resumes for job openings and the use of a software program offers the company a way to reduce the amount of resumes that are even seen by the person that is doing the hiring. As these bots are designed to search out key words that are often included in the job description, it will be important for you to place some of these keywords in your resume. Second, if the company or person doing the hiring has listed specific traits or things they are looking for from an applicant and these things are applicable to you, then you should make sure to reinforce these keywords in telling the prospective employer why you would be well-suited for the job. For example, if the job posting says that the employer is looking for a "self-motivated individual" you might mention in your resume that although you can take direction very well, you are also self-motivated to the point where you can take a project and run with it. In using some of the job descriptions

keywords, you'll not only be showing them that you read their posting, but, more importantly, that you are the right person for the job.

8) **Optimize and organize information.** I always tell job applicants to limit their resumes to two pages maximum; possibly one page, depending on the job they are applying for. In organizing your information, it's important that you place the most pertinent information near the top of the resume. For example, if a person has been working for 20 years and they graduated from college 20 years ago, their educational background is probably going to be a lot less pertinent than their work experience. Thus, education information should appear lower in the resume. Or, if a person is applying for a restaurant marketing job, and they have previously had a restaurant marketing job with another company even though that may not have been their most recent job, it might be appropriate to list that restaurant experience nearer to the top of the resume than the non-restaurant related job experience.

How to Tailor Your Resume to a Specific Job.

If you want to enhance the chances to get an interview for the jobs you're applying for, you're almost certainly going to have to tailor your resume to the specific job you're applying for. If you don't do that, the company or person who is hiring is likely to presume that you aren't very interested in their job opening and you're likely to fall toward the bottom of the resume pile.

Once you have all of the basic information on your resume template form, it will be much easier to adapt this information to fit any job you are applying for.

Job Search

There are some simple ways you can customize your resume to fit the job you are applying for:

1) **Identify the things that are important to the employer.** You can do this by reading the job description. What things does the employer say they are looking for in an employee? What qualities or traits appear near the top of the ad? These are likely to be more important than qualities or traits that appear near the bottom of the ad. Does the job post mention anything a number of times or repetitively? If so, this is probably something that is particularly important to the employer.

2) **Once you've identified the things that appear to be important** to the employer in the job listing, you should then match these things with the various things listed on your resume. For example, if the job post emphasizes that they want to hire someone who has leadership abilities, you should find experiences in your background in which you had to lead others. Even if you haven't previously mentioned leadership on your resume, you should review your past experiences to see if you had any leadership roles and then, if so, add those experiences to your tailored resume. Or maybe the employer is looking to hire someone who is a good multi-tasker. Do you have any examples to add to your resume that show that you are a capable multi-tasker? If so, please emphasize this on your resume. It will not be enough to just list that you are good at multi-tasking on your resume. Most employers will be able to see through this. You should give specific examples of your multi-tasking experience. In tailoring your resume, it will behoove you to be as specific as possible. If you're interviewing for a sales position and you've had previous

success in a sales position, you could mention that sales percentage increase you had in that previous position. If you are interviewing for a management position, you could mention that you managed a staff of 14 people in your previous job and/or that you hired and trained four new employees in that position. The more specific you can be, the more believable you'll be with the examples you're giving.

3) **Add/remove/reorder/modify.** In tailoring your resume to a specific job, it is important that you remain flexible in adapting your resume. Don't hesitate to move elements of your resume around, including the order of the items shown. If something from your resume is not at all pertinent with this job, don't hesitate to remove it. And if, based on the description in the job post, you find any other parcels from your background that might help you get an interview, you should add those items to your resume. Again, you don't want your resume to become too long, so if you are adding some parcels, you might delete others. If you can't fit all the information that you want in the resume itself, you might consider placing any pertinent extra information in your cover letter.

4) **Use the tailored resume to prepare for your interview.** If you're fortunate enough to secure an interview based on your tailored resume, you'll be able to use that information to determine talking points or points of emphasis in your interview. For example, if the person interviewing you asks you to tell them about yourself or to tell you why you are interested in their job, you will be able to use those talking points to answer those questions, knowing full well what is important to them in their search for an employee. Instead of

rambling on about things that may not be important to them, you should be able to pinpoint the areas they are interested in. That should enhance your chances for success in any interview.

How to Write Great Cover Letters.

Whenever you get the opportunity, you should write a cover letter to accompany your resume. Cover letters will allow you a chance to expand and go beyond your resume. The goal of a cover letter should be to get the person reading it to want to review your resume and hopefully to get a quick glimpse as to why you are a good candidate for the open position. Here are some random tips, techniques, and thoughts for writing an effective cover letter. Although not all of these tips may apply to your particular cover letter, these ideas will give you some things to consider in drafting your letter.

1) **Try to limit your cover letter to one page.** Certainly, never more than two pages.

2) **If possible, address the cover letter to the attention of the person who Is doing the hiring.** If you do this, make sure you have the correct spelling of the person whose name you are using. You can decide whether you want to use a more formal reference such as Ms. or Mr. I generally prefer less casual, such as first names. However, if you are using a first name, you should probably do some research as to what first name the person goes by. For example, does someone named Charles go by Charles, Charlie, Chaz, or Chuck? Does James go by James, Jim, or Jimmy? If you are going to

use a first name, I suggest you make sure of their name preference. If you're not sure of the name the hirer goes by, a simple phone call to the receptionist at the company should provide the necessary information. Simply tell them that you want to send correspondence to this person and find out what their name preference is.

3) **Your tone in a cover letter should be conversational instead of formal.** Whereas your resume should be formal, your cover letter should be much less formal. Cover letters offer you the opportunity to "write between the lines", telling the reader who are you as a person, telling them why you are interested in the job they are offering, and telling them why you are a good fit for that job. When you are writing your cover letters, you should use a conversational tone. In other words, write it as you would say it, as if you are having a conversation with the person who is reading it. In doing this, you'll be able to show your prospective employer that you are much more than just a formal list of resume credentials.

4) **With your cover letter, you'll need to do more than to simply highlight or rehash the information that you included on your accompanying resume.**

5) **Use your cover letter as a chance to expand upon one or some of the talking points in your resume.** Expand upon why you are the right person for the job, maybe highlighting in further detail some of your experiences or accomplishments. For example, if the company's job description states that it is important for the applicant to

be a self-starter, you should highlight the fact that you work well with or without supervision and that you can take a project from start to finish without a lot of supervision. If the company is looking for someone who can multi-task and work on multiple projects at the same time, you should highlight any past experience you've had with that. Here's an excerpt from one of my clients, who was applying for a public relations job which required attention to multiple projects at the same time: "Your job description notes that this position will require the ability to multi-task. As a public relations associate for IDQ, I coordinated many projects at the same time, including the company's milk carton boat race sponsorship, the company's systemwide support of the National Kidney Foundation, the company's Run, Hit, and Throw youth baseball competition, and the coordination of press conferences announcing the introduction of the company's new institutional foods program. All were major public relations programs that I handled successfully." As you'll note by this excerpt, the applicant certainly provided proof that they could handle multiple projects concurrently. And I like that fact that they were very specific in detailing those projects. Much better than just saying "I'm able to multi-task" and leaving it at that.

6) **If possible, your opening line should be one that will grab the attention of the reader.** Although it's important to grab the reader's attention, I wouldn't do so at the risk of being corny or hokey. You might incorporate your experience, your passion, or your past accomplishments into the opening sentence. For example, here's the opening lines of a cover letter that

someone wrote with an application for a Barnes & Noble bookseller job: "Over the years, I've spent a lot of time in your Barnes & Noble bookstore. I'm an avid reader and I love the Barnes & Noble concept. With this passion and knowledge of books and with my penchant for great customer service, I feel like I'll be a great fit for your opening for a bookseller." With these opening lines, you'll note that the applicant mentions the job he is applying for, he compliments the company, he explains how he will fit within that company with his passion for books, and he also details that he is good at customer service. In just three sentences, he's given the reader some reasons why he should be near the top of the resume pile.

If you can't think of anything in particular to grab the reader, then I suggest that you go with something more generic, such as, "I'm excited to apply for your marketing associate position at ABC Company. I've read some articles regarding your company and visited your company web site and, with my experience and enthusiasm, I think I can become a valuable asset there."

7) **As you'll note by the previous sentence, the applicant is outlining what he can do for the company instead of what the company can do for him.** You should avoid mentioning what the company can do for you, as the person who is hiring already knows what the company can do for you.

8) **In any cover letter, you should outline the things you can "bring to the party".** How can you become an asset to the company that is hiring. If you have experiences,

expertise, or knowledge that will allow you to become an asset there, you should mention those things in your cover letter. Even if you don't have much experience to bring to the table, you can certainly mention less tangent things such as energy, enthusiasm, passion, the willingness to learn, the willingness to work hard, etc.

9) **If you have numbers to prove your case, use them.** For example, a friend of mine who was applying for a sales job listed numbers from his previous sales job in which he was the top salesperson from a salesforce of 9. His sales accounted for 36% of company sales, he brought in 20% of the company's new customers, and he won Salesperson of the Year each of the three years he was there. Another example, for someone who was applying for a supervisory position in which the person who be responsible for hiring, training, and managing a staff of about 10 people, the applicant mentioned that she had successfully hired and trained a department of seven accountants or accounting assistants, and her department had the lowest turnover rate of any department within the company.

10) **Testimonials.** If you have any testimonials or testaments to your abilities or talents, a cover letter is a good place to use them. Going back to the aforementioned accounting supervisor, she used the following testimonial in her cover letter. "One of the employees I hired and trained, told me that I was the fourth boss she had and that I was the first boss who had taken the time with her to make her a valuable employee. She later became our department's employee of the year and she later told me

that the help I had given her had a major impact on her career." Again, these testimonials are things that you normally would not include in a resume, however they work well in cover letters and they might well help differentiate you from other applicants and get you to the top of the resume pile.

11) **Don't be afraid to pat yourself on the back**. A cover letter is a good place to trumpet your previous achievements or accomplishments. Remember, if you don't toot your own horn during the interview process, no one else is going to do that for you.

12) **Finish strong.** Your final sentence or final paragraph of your resume will be your last shot at making an impression with the reader. Make sure you finish strong, possible reiterating why you would like to work for the company, what you can bring to the table, or why you would be a good fit. And again, if you don't have any tangible assets, maybe because you're applying for your first job or you're new to the workforce, you can always promise that you are willing to learn or to work hard to become a valued asset of the company.

13) **Edit and review.** It almost goes without saying that you need to check your cover letter (and resume) for spelling, grammar, and punctuation errors. I know people who hire who will discard perfectly good candidates due to spelling or grammar errors, even if spelling and grammar are unrelated to the job opening. Some people view these

areas as carelessness, lack of attention to detail, etc. So, I'd recommend that you use spell-check to check your content. Also, if you know people who can read your resume and cover letter to then provide feedback before it goes to the prospective employer, you should ask for their assistance.

Again, the goal of any cover letter is to get the reader to read the accompanying resume. The goal of a resume is to get you an interview. The goal of both the cover letter and the resume are to separate you from all of the other applicants for the same opening. Keep this in mind when writing your cover letter. If it is so blah that it doesn't make an impression, you probably won't get an interview.

Chapter 3 - Get Ahead with an Online Portfolio

If you want to enhance your chances to get jobs or projects, you should consider having an online presence, if you don't already have one. If you can build your own personal brand online, you'll be able to supplement any resume or cover letter you send out. And you can do so very economically, even for free.

Before we delve deeper into what you can do to establish an online presence that will help you get the job of your dreams, let's briefly discuss the online presence you already have, especially in regards to social media.

Before you embark upon your job search, I strongly suggest that you review your social media presence and make sure none of that image will impact your ability to get a job. It's no secret that many employers will look you up on social media before extending a job offer. I've had job search clients who have lost job opportunities because of their online presence. One of my clients was a recent college grad whose Facebook page was full of party photos, some of which showed him in what looked to be a drunken state. Another of my clients had a Facebook page which was riddled by inappropriate language; another had a page which was laced with political rants. Certainly, these items should have been cleaned up before they embarked on their job search. In searching for a job, you should presume that your prospective employer will check to see what kind of an online presence you have, including platforms such as Facebook, Instagram, Twitter, etc.

Also, they will probably do a Google search on you to see if there are any stories or blurbs about you on the internet. There may be things about you on the internet that you can't delete or clean up. But you should at least know what information about you is readily available on the internet and then if any of that information is negative, you should probably have an explanation for that information, as you may be asked about it by a prospective employer. I had a young client who was arrested for breaking and entering into a golf clubhouse when he was 17. His name appeared in the small town newspaper and that information remains on the internet and is something that still haunts him even years later. He has an unusual name, so there is no doubt that he was involved in the crime. So, now he is prepared to expound on this incident if asked about it by prospective employers. Honesty is his best policy in explaining that it was a dumb adolescent mistake that he deeply regrets and will not repeat.

So, the bottom line is that before you start your job search, make sure you take a look at your social media presence. Look at it through the eyes of a prospective employer and make sure that it's not going to impact you negatively. If so, correct whatever you can correct and be prepared to explain whatever you can't correct.

Tips for Building an Online Portfolio That Gets You Hired.

Now that you've reviewed and filtered the online presence you already have, you can move forward and establish a presence that will assist you in your job search efforts. Depending on your profession or the job you are looking to secure, you'll have to figure out whether you want to have a graphic presence, a written presence, or both. If you are a commercial artist, a photographer, a graphic designer, a cake decorator, an event planner, those are professions or vocations that are conducive toward a visual presence on the internet. If you are a freelance writer, a household budgeting expert, or a relationship counselor, those professions are conducive to a written presence on the internet, possibly a blog presence. LinkedIn is a business and employment-oriented platform that is probably the most popular means to establish an online professional presence. We'll discuss that platform specifically later in the chapter. But for now, I'd like to inform you about other possible ways you can create an online professional presence or brand.

1) **Web site**. These days, setting up a simple web site is quite easy. You don't need to be a coder and you should be able to set it up yourself if you are even a bit tech savvy. Sites such as Squarespace, Wix, HostGator, and GoDaddy are all web site hosts that have inexpensive site hosting that range in price from free to $15 per month, depending on the features you want. All of these sites are geared toward consumers who want to set up simple web sites and they offer simple instructions on how to do so. In having your own personal web site, you can promote some of your skills. My daughter-in-law is a wedding planner and she has a simple web site which contains photos of the different weddings she has planned over the years. This web site is vital to her business and she has obtained numerous gigs as a result of the web site. I have a client who is a graphic artist who also has his own site. On the site, he has posted samples of some of the projects he's done and he uses the site as a portfolio for his talents and abilities. Although he is a freelancer now, he previously used a similar web site to get his job as a corporate artist.

If any of your areas of expertise are conducive to visual representation, I suggest you consider creating your own web site to promote and display your talents. In doing so, you should also make sure you have an About You section in which you tell a bit about yourself. You can use this page as an extension of your resume, although it should be a lot less formal and more conversational. You can convey as much information as you'd like, but you should remember that your viewers will be typical web browsers who will spend a minimal amount of time on each page. So, there's no need to write a book about yourself for this section of the web site.

    2) **Blogs.** Maybe your area of expertise is more verbal than graphic. If so, you might consider creating a blog to promote yourself. Again, there are many inexpensive blog platforms available to you, including Wix, Squarespace, and WordPress. Monthly hosting charges are very nominal, and this a great way to advertise your talents and expertise. As an example, I have a friend of mine who makes her living as a professional dog trainer. She writes a monthly blog which includes stories and tips about dog training. With her blog, she has established herself as an expert in the field. You can do the same with your blog. Another friend of mine is a freelance writer who has samples of about 25 different pieces she has written on her blog site. So, in searching for a job, you can direct a prospective employer to your blog site and they'll be able to spend as much time there as they would like in reading your blogs.

If you are not a proficient writer by trade, that shouldn't necessarily discourage you from having a blog, as you can hire freelance writers who can do that for you, often inexpensively. Upwork is a freelance platform on which you can have blogs written anywhere from $15 to $50 per blog. In hiring a freelancer, you should remember that they can only be as good as the information you give them, so be prepared to furnish them with an outline of the information you want contained in the blog.

    3) **YouTube.** Maybe your talent or area of expertise is better shown in video format. If so, you should consider posting

some short video clips on YouTube. I have quite a few clients who have established themselves as experts in their fields by posting video tutorials on YouTube. I know two people who are information technology gurus who post video clips regarding how to solve various computer problems for people who are not tech-oriented. The guy who does my small engine repair (lawnmower, vacuum cleaner) has a series of video tutorials on Facebook, as does my appliance repairman. With these tutorials, it should be pointed out that they are not necessarily professionally done, as a television infomercial would be. These tutorials are simply done, by one person, no production crew. The information provided is much more important than the production quality and these short videos establish the creators as experts in their field. You can do the same thing in establishing yourself as an expert in your field and this can definitely help as you search for a job.

When a prospective employer is searching job candidates, you'll be able to vault to the top of the resume pile if you can show them that you are an expert in your field or good at what you do. As you may find out in your own job search, getting the job of your dreams often involves a lot more than just having a resume and a cover letter. You'll want to make sure that you have a professional presence on the internet.

The Lowdown on Creating an Irresistible LinkedIn Profile.

If you're looking to find a job or if you're looking to increase your professional visibility or establish your professional brand, using LinkedIn is a "must". LinkedIn is the largest online professional networking site. It is a platform that many employers and recruiters use in securing job candidates. A platform that is geared toward professionals, LinkedIn offers professionals the opportunity to network, to search job openings or job candidates, and for members to showcase their professional abilities, talents, accomplishments, and achievements.

I've compiled some simple tips and techniques which you can use to establish a top-notch presence on LinkedIn. This information should be beneficial to you as you create or enhance your LinkedIn profile.

1) **The more complete, the better.** In establishing your LinkedIn profile, you'll want to make sure that you complete every section of the profile. A prospective employer is likely to frown upon a candidate who does not have a complete profile. And in completing your profile, please make sure you tell people what your skills are and where you've worked.

2) **Use a conversational, passionate, optimistic tone.** With the information you include in your LinkedIn profile, you should always use a conversational, somewhat casual tone. Hopefully, you'll be able to convey some of your personality with your LinkedIn profile. Remember that any prospective employer will be looking at numerous profiles and you'll want to make sure that this person gets a quick feel for your personality as they read your profile. Always use the first person (I or me) when referring to yourself. And be sure to show your enthusiasm or passion toward what you do or what you want to do. For example, with my friend who was seeking a bookselling job, he included his passion in his profile: "I love books. I love reading them, I love discussing them, I love sharing them with others, and I'm sure I'll love selling them." With just this short statement, the reader understands quickly that this person is a booklover. His passion shows immediately.

3) **Show numbers if you have them.** Besides showing passion, show numbers. Prospective employers often like numbers, something tangible to rate your abilities. If you are a graphic artist, you might mention that you've done over 400 projects for over 70 different clients. And that your retention rate for your customers is over 95%. If you're in the advertising business, you might mention that one of the ad campaigns you designed produced a 300% sales increase when the goal had been a 25% increase. Anything you can do to correlate tangible numbers with your accomplishments will make you look better in the eyes of anyone who might be interested in hiring you.

4) **Use a great photo of yourself.** Although this might seem obvious, some people make the mistake of not posting a good photo in conjunction with their profile. In your photo, you should be dressed appropriately for your position or the position your interested in. And, if you can, it will be good if you can use a photo which shows you in action. For example, if you have guest speaking experience and you have a photo of you talking to an audience, that may well be preferable to just a plain headshot. Or if you are a corporate attorney, you might post a photo of you meeting with a client or inside a courtroom.

5) **Write an attention-grabbing headline.** Again, remembering that any prospective employer will be looking at multiple profiles, it will be important for you to grab the viewer's attention as soon as possible, hopefully with an attention-grabbing headline. As an example, a friend of mine who is a freelance writer who offers quick turnaround has used a "Fastest Pen in the West" headline for her profile. Anything

you can do to separate yourself from other candidates will give you a better chance to get the job you're looking for.

6) **Add multi-media to your profile**. LinkedIn profiles offer you the opportunity to "show and tell" your talents, abilities, experiences, and achievements. Any samples you can show to tell prospective employers why you are the person for the job or why you are an expert in your field will increase your chances in getting the job of your dreams. And, as we all know, people love visual accompaniments. With this in mind, you should see if you can enhance your LinkedIn profile by adding accompaniments such as photos, video clips, blogs, or slideshows. Again, these should all be related to your professional career, with the goal of showcasing your talents or expertise. In most instances, these visual aides should be placed in the summary area of your profile.

You can also enhance your profile by providing links to any articles about you or photos of you on the internet, even if it's just a mention for a professional achievement. If you have been an employee for a company that is not well-known, you might also provide a link to that company's web site, so the prospective employer can get an idea of who you worked for. In providing links to your professional achievements or your previous places of employment, you'll also be directing any searches that prospective employers might be doing on you.

7) **Connections**. With your LinkedIn profile, you should also know that it will be important for you to have a significant number of connections. As a rule of thumb, you should try to have at least 50 connections. Anything less than that may be a red flag to prospective employers who may think you're a hermit, you're anti-social or simply not interested in connecting with others, you're not technology- or social media-oriented, or you're just not a viable candidate. In

establishing connections, you should remember that it's not a contest to see who has the most connections, however you want to at least have enough connections to establish your credibility. Don't add people you don't know. If you have enough people who are rejecting your connection requests because they say they don't know you, LinkedIn reserves the right to shut down your profile.

8) **Keep your job search confidential.** If you have a current job, you might not want your current employer to know that you're looking to find another job. If this is the case, you can use the LinkedIn privacy settings to make sure that your current employer doesn't know that you are looking to find another job.

9) **Make sure people know how to find you.** Just a quick reminder to make sure that your resume includes your contact information. (email address, Twitter handle, blog, etc.—someplace you check for messages, at least on a daily basis.) You'd be surprised how many people forget to include this simple and pertinent information on their resumes.

10) **Request recommendations**. It will be important for you to have recommendations from current and former business associates. Don't be shy in asking your contacts to provide testimonials. And if you have any particular area or subject for which you'd like them to provide the testimonial, don't hesitate to tell them what subject you'd like them to broach. And, remember, you can control/select the recommendations you show on your profile. So, you can use these recommendations to show whatever areas of strength or expertise your interested in, and you can change these on an on-going basis as you adjust your preferences.

11) **Groups.** One of the best features of LinkedIn is that it has LinkedIn Groups that can be invaluable in helping you to secure a job within your industry. By joining groups which are related to your industry or profession, you'll be able to show that you are involved and engaged in that industry and you'll be able to connect to people who have access to information about job openings, industry trends or talking points, etc. These LinkedIn groups offer ongoing, online network opportunities which you can utilize in your job search.

12) **Always include current job listing, even if unemployed.** As most prospective employers use only the current title box on LinkedIn to look for candidates, it's important that you list a current position in the experience section of your profile. If you're unemployed, you should simply list your most recent position or the position or field you're looking for and then follow that with a further title description in the company name box. As an example, you can list the following: Graduating student/marketing major. List that in the current job title box. And then in the company name box, list "In transition" or "Seeking career opportunities". Either way, it's important to make sure you don't leave the current job box empty, so employers who are searching only the current title box section will be able to access your profile.

How a Blog Can Boost Your Career.

Earlier in this chapter, I mentioned that having a blog can be an excellent means of placing you above the clutter of candidates in your efforts to find a job. I'll now expound upon why a blog can be an important tool in helping you get that job you want to get.

Blogs can be used to complement your resume. Although a resume outlines your previous work and education experiences, a blog can be used to expand on that. As resumes are somewhat restrictive in the amount of information they can contain, blogs allow you to showcase your knowledge and expertise. They can provide prospective employers with a better look into who you are and what your talents and abilities are.

Blogs allow you to establish yourself as an expert or leader in your field. They also provide an excellent means for you to build and promote your personal brand. In having a blog, you'll also establish that fact that you have a digital footprint—you're internet and social media savvy and you know how to use technology to promote yourself and to reach others. A blog will also show that you have passion and pride in your career or profession.

As resumes and cover letters are traditionally restricted in length to two pages or less, blogs offer a great way for you to expound on your experience and convey who you are to prospective employers. Employers and recruiters are always looking for ways to differentiate job candidates from each other.

In establishing a blog, I suggest that you have at least three or four blogs available for reading immediately after you start your blogs. One blog is not enough to give the reader an idea as to your areas of expertise. You'll want at least a few blogs to retain the reader. And then after your initial postings, I would recommend that you add a new blog at least once a month, hopefully at the same time each month. Ideally, you will have a registration mechanism on your blog site that allows you to send them notifications as to when your blogs are available on your hosting site. An average blog length goes from 500 to 1000 words, although you can certainly use any length for your blogs. Again, if you are not a proficient writer, but have valuable information to disseminate, you can always hire a freelance writer to write your blogs for you. This can be done inexpensively. If you're hiring a freelancer to write your blog, you should remember that a freelancer is only as good as the information you provide to him or her.

Six Fabulous Tools to Help You Put Together Your Online Portfolio.

Here are some additional tools for you to use in developing your online portfolio. We've mentioned some of these tools before; others may be new to you.

1) **LinkedIn**. We've already discussed this at length, however I want to mention it again, because it's a vital tool for you to use in establishing your online portfolio. You can add visuals, videos, audios, and files. And it's free.

2) **Vizualize.me.** A solid platform that allows you to choose from a multitude of different themes and styles to chronicle your career in a visual format. Connects to LinkedIn.

3) **Personal web sites.** Lots of web site concepts to choose from, including Weebly, Wix, Squarespace, GoDaddy, and HostGator. These sites, which are either free or available at a nominal price, all allow professionals to build their own personal sites quickly and easily. Most of these concepts have many different stock templates and styles for you to choose from in designing a site that fits you, your personality, and your experience.

Job Search

4) **About.me.** This site offers a simple way for anyone to build a landing page that includes images and brief text.

5) **Blog sites.** WordPress, Squarespace, and Wix are among sites that special in personal blog hosting. All offer different design templates for you to choose from.

6) **PortfolioBox.** This is a portfolio design platform that works particularly well for professional people who have a lot of visual items to display. This includes photographers, graphic designers, and artists, who can show lots of samples of their works on the platform. Thousands of themes to choose from. Optimized for smartphone and tablet viewing. Also great for other business professional who have a lot of visual to show.

As you can see, there are many different tools and platforms available for you to establish an online professional presence that supplements your resume. If you want to get to the top of the pack as a job candidate, the best way to ensure that will be to establish an impressive online presence, where you can convey your talents and abilities to a prospective employer who is looking to find the difference between all job candidates.

Chapter 4—Networking for Success

Before I fully understood the concept of networking, I was reluctant to do it. I always had the idea that if I networked, I would come across as being self-serving, pushy, and maybe even annoying. But then a friend of mine put networking into a different perspective for me, telling me that networking is simply the concept of keeping my eyes open and building better relationship whenever possible, with the people I know and also with people I don't know. Hands down, networking can be one of the most effective means of getting a job.

The fundamentals of networking. Just as the mantra of successful real estate is "location, location, location", the mantra of successful networking is "connect, connect, connect". You may not realize it, but you already have your own network. Whether it is your business associates, your old high school and college friends, the parents of your kids' schoolmates, people who are in your volunteer group, or the people you play pickup basketball with, all of these people are people who could help you get your next job.

It's important to remember a couple of things in regards to networking. First of all, you should know that people prefer to do business with people they have some kind of connection to. Resumes and cover letters are important, however they're often too impersonal to get someone to hire you. Second, as we've mentioned before, most job listings get lots of applicants. With this in mind, you'll need a point of difference that can place you above the other people applying for the same job. Finally, you should note that many jobs are not advertised. Networking can result in job leads that you will not get through regular job search channels. Maybe these jobs will never be advertised or maybe they've yet to be advertised and you'll get a jump on the job posting.

Before you begin networking, you should make a list of the people in your network. In doing this, you'll surely find that this list is much larger than you thought it would be. In listing your contacts, you should include family, friends, neighbors, co-workers and colleagues, high school and college schoolmates, social media contacts, email contacts, and casual acquaintances. And don't forget other people you do business with on a regular basis, including your doctor, your dentist, your dry cleaner, your pharmacist, your yoga instructor, your landlord, your accountant, etc. And likewise, don't forget other people you come into contact with on a regular basis, including fellow civic members, health club members, volunteer group members, church members, etc.

Always remember that each member of a network has the capability to provide invaluable information about a job opening or they may know someone who can help. Don't ignore anyone. A client of mine, who is a restaurant marketing executive, first found out about the opening for the job he now has through his dry cleaner. Yes, dry cleaners and marketing execs probably run in different circles, however the dry cleaner had a brother-in-law who worked for a restaurant chain that was getting ready to advertise for a marketing position. The networking between the marketing exec and the dry cleaner was plain and simple. When the dry cleaner asked the marketing exec how he was doing, the marketing exec mentioned that he was between jobs and he was looking for a restaurant marketing job. Ironically, the dry cleaner's brother-in-law worked for a restaurant chain and that's how the networking all started. The dry cleaner called his brother-in-law, confirmed the opening he had heard about when he was visiting his sister and brother-in-law, he confirmed the opening and then he put his dry cleaning customer (the restaurant marketing exec) in touch with his brother-in-law. The ball started rolling, and three weeks later, after three interviews, the marketing exec had a job he had been looking for.

In getting people into the networking mode, I always encourage them to develop a networking mindset. I tell them to "keep their eyes and their minds" open, to presume that anyone they meet can provide them with information that will help them to get their next job. And you should approach networking as a concept that is fun, even if you have an agenda. If you consider networking as burdensome, you're not going to do it. But if you go in with a positive attitude, you'll find that you enjoy connecting or reconnecting with people. Also, if you're unemployed or employed in a job that you don't like, you'll benefit from the support system offered by networking. Looking for a good job can often be depressing and you'll enjoy the encouragement and emotional support you can get from networking.

If you're going to be a good networker, you can't go through life with blinders on. You'll need to consider just about every person you meet as a candidate to help you in your job search.

Yes, there is an art to asking for help. Many of the daily interactions we have are very brief and you'll have to figure out a way to ask for help without coming across as pushy or overly aggressive. You'll have to figure out a style which fits your personality, but you can do that with practice.

In asking for job leads or information, you should remember that most people love to be helpful. It feels good to help others; you'll find that people will be glad to help you if they can. Anyone who has helped someone else realizes the satisfaction you can receive in doing that. Also, remember that people generally love to give advice and they like to be asked to give advice. It's natural that people like to be recognized for their expertise and for their potential to help others.

Job Search

Whether you are unemployed, stuck in a crappy job or a low-paying job, you should remember that at one time or another, your network contacts have probably been in the same position. They'll be empathetic to your situation and, as a result, they'll be quick to help if they can.

And remember, networking is a two-way street. If you're going to ask for help, you should also be prepared to help the person you're asking for help. There's an old saying, "If you scratch my back, I'll scratch yours." That's a saying that describes the concept of networking. Networking is not just about helping yourself. It is also about helping others. As another saying goes, "Give and you shall receive."

After you've assembled your networking list, it's time for you to start "working" that list. If you're looking for networking assistance in finding a job, it makes sense that you should inform as many people as possible about your job search. Of course, if you already have a job and are looking for another, you're most likely going to have to have some discretion as you advertise the fact that you're looking for a new job. You might impair your chances of keeping your current job if you are openly advertising for another job. But if you're unemployed and find that there won't be any negative consequences in advertising that you are looking for a new job, I suggest that you start contacting as many people as possible as quickly as you can. Please remember that no one can help you find a new job if they don't know you are looking for one.

You should come up with a game plan on how you're going to ask for help from your network. If you're unemployed, you might consider informing your network of your search by posting a note on your social media platforms. You can do the same with your email contact list. And, with some people, you'll want to contact them personally by calling them, messaging them, or connecting with them in whatever means possible.

In requesting help in getting a job, the more specific you can be, the better off you'll be. Instead of the old "let me know if you hear of anything" line, you should be more specific in requesting help. If you are looking for an accounting job with a large accounting firm, you should mention that. If you are looking for a marketing position with a restaurant chain or a franchised chain, you should mention that.

And always keep your network updated on your progress in getting a job, especially those networkers who try to help you in your efforts. Let them know whether you got an interview or a job resulting from the information they offered. Always thank your networkers, regardless of the outcome and whether or not you got the interview or the job. I have a number of clients who update their networkers of their progress on a weekly basis through an email. One of those clients has even established a theme for her updates. She calls it "Finding a Job for Lisa" and sends out a humorous and light-hearted update to her network every week. In doing this, she continues to remind her networkers of her job search and she also gets them to invest in her efforts and success in finding a job.

I always caution people not to become "hit and run" networkers or "here today, gone tomorrow" networkers. It's important to continue to network even after you land a job. Again, networking is a two-way street and if someone is helpful, you shouldn't just take their help and run. The goal is to continue to network, as you never know when you'll need to use your network again. Also, you should offer to reciprocate any of the help you receive. If you can ever help someone in your network, you should do so. And, by all means, don't forget to thank those people who help you in any way.

One other thing I'd like to mention regarding the fundamentals of networking. You should prioritize your contacts and then decide on who you'll use as your references. In selecting possible job and personal references, you should obviously make sure that they will give you a reference that will allow you to secure the job you're hoping to get. I had a client who had difficulty in getting a job a few years ago. He went through a number of interviews, but could never land the job. In some of the interviews, he even got to the stage in which the prospective employer was calling his references. Finally, my client called one of the employers he had interviewed with and asked them why he didn't get the job offer that he had been expected. The employer hinted strongly that my client needed to double-check his references. My client later figured which one of his references had been providing "less than glowing" references and had, in fact, sabotaged my client's job search. To this day, my client still isn't sure whether these mediocre or negative references were intentional or not. But he quickly deleted this reference from his list as he proceeded with his job search.

As you embark on your job search, you should make sure you ask your prospective references if they will vouch for you. With a phone call or a personal meeting, you can hopefully tell them what you are looking for and tell them what points you'd like them to highlight in acting as a reference for you. Also, you may want to keep them posted by sending them copies of your resume and cover letters, so you can make sure they are up-to-date with your job search efforts and also to get them to be more invested in your job search. Whether you send them a resume or not, it's important that you keep your references in the loop regarding your job search.

Ten Networking Questions to Ask. If you're new to networking or if you're not comfortable to do networking, I've listed some questions you might ask of the people you're networking with. When people ask me about the best ways to network, I always tell them that the most important thing to do in talking with another networker is to "be engaged". No, I'm not talking about a prospective marital situation, but I'm encouraging you to "be interested" in the conversation you're having. Give the person you're talking to your undivided attention. A number of years ago, I attended a networking event with a friend of mine and I was surprised to note that my longtime friend was doing a poor job of connecting to the people he was talking to. He wasn't making eye contact and he kept looking over the shoulder of the person he was talking to (maybe trying to identify the person he would talk to next). All in all, he seemed to be very disengaged and distracted. He definitely wasn't invested in the conversation he was having and I was sure the people he was talking to picked up on his lack of engagement.

After the networking event, I mentioned my observations to my friend, who I've always thought to have a short attention span. He was surprised that I had noticed this deficiency and he resolved to change his mode of operation. Months later when he and I talked, he told me that he had been to two subsequent networking events and he had made it a point to give the people he was talking to his undivided attention. He was pleased to tell me that he had already noticed that he was having more success as a networker. So, bottom line, when you're networking, make sure you are engaged with the people you're talking to.

Here are some questions you might use when you're networking with people who you don't already know:
1) **What do you do for a living?**
2) **Do you enjoy it?**
3) **How did you get into that? Did you have previous experience? Did you study that?**
4) **What company do you work for? How long have you worked for them? Is that a good place to work?**
5) **What's your favorite part of your job? What projects are you working on now?**
6) **What's next for you? Any career goals and objectives?**

7) **What do you like to do outside of work? Any interests or hobbies?**
8) **Do you do much networking?**
9) **Would you like to keep in touch?**
10) **How Can I Help?**

I love the "How Can I Help?" attitude. There's a popular television show on NBC called "New Amsterdam" in which the head of the New Amsterdam hospital has adopted the "How Can I Help?" mantra in his interactions with both staff and patients. Instead of just telling people what to do, he makes a point to always ask them how he can help. The people you're networking with are sure to appreciate your offer to help them with their careers and you'll likely make a great impression if you can adopt this attitude. However, please make sure you are sincere with your offer to help. And if you offer to do something for a fellow networker, you should make sure you follow through on your promises. Hollow promises or lip service without the follow through will be sure to tarnish your reputation as a networker.

In asking questions of fellow networkers, you'll find quickly that most people like to talk about themselves. And, in asking questions, don't have a firm set of questions to ask every one you speak with. Go with the flow of the conversation and let the direction of the conversation go wherever it takes you. A friend of mine was a member of a dating site and he recently had his first and only date with a woman who pulled out a written set of questions to ask him. Ultimately, he felt very uncomfortable with the situation and said that he felt like he was being interrogated. You won't want to do this when you are networking. Let the conversation take you where it takes you. Remember, networking is meant to be a casual activity, not an interrogation.

In asking questions of fellow networkers, you'll quickly find that asking questions will soon come naturally. And, chances are, if you become a proficient networker, you'll also become great at asking questions of prospective employers during interviews. Again, remember that people like to talk about themselves and if you can ask them the right questions, you will often find that people will think they had a great conversation, even if they did most of the talking.

How to Network If You're an Introvert. Studies show that about one-third of all people can be categorized as introverts. If you're an introvert, you may not look forward to networking. But, despite your concerns, introverts can still be proficient networkers. If you're an introvert, the most important thing for you to do in networking is for you to be yourself. Don't try to be someone you're not. You don't have to be the life of the party. You can get noticed and be an effective networker by being yourself.

I find that many introverts prefer smaller groups or one-on-one interactions. If you're an introvert, you might focus your attention to these smaller meetings or interactions, as you might well get lost within a larger group. And if you're at a networking event, remember that you're not the only person there who is scared or who is an introvert. You're not alone. With this in mind, you should note that there will be other introverts at the event who you can interact with. Introverts are often easy to identify. Kind of like wallflowers at a high school dance, you can probably identify introverts as those people who are off by themselves in a corner feeling awkward or buried in a large group and saying nothing. If necessary, you can gravitate toward other introverts, who will likely welcome your company. And remember, just because a person is an introvert doesn't mean that they don't have valuable contacts or have valuable information which can help you in your job search.

Another way for an introvert to be more successful at networking events is to find a "networking buddy", someone who can walk around with you as you meet other networkers. Introverts will often find it helpful to have a wingman or wingwoman. Even if you don't have a wingman, if you know someone else at the networking event, you should not hesitate to ask them to introduce you to other networkers. This should eliminate a lot of the initial awkwardness of being introduced to someone new.

And when you meet people, as mentioned earlier in this chapter, make sure you stay engaged in your conversation. Be there. Keep your phone in your pocket. Listen to what they say.

I know some introverts who even practice for networking events by coming up with a mental list of questions to ask the people they meet. This will help dispense with some of the stuttering and stammering which can often occur in meeting someone new.

I also encourage people, especially introverts, to set goals and objectives before any networking event. For example, one of my clients, always sets a goal to meet four new people and to connect with four other people he already knows at each networking event. If he can do this, he feels like he has been a successful networker for that event.

And, when you're at a networking event, make sure you don't wear out your welcome. After you've talked to someone for a while, be aware that you don't want to take up too much of their time, and move on to another networker. It's not prudent to dominate all of one person's time. After all, it is a networking event, and the goal is to meet a number of different people.

And, finally, in regards to introverts, I should mention that many introverts use the internet to network with other people. This includes people they don't yet know. You can meet new people online through professional network groups like those offered by LinkedIn. And, with people you already know, you can continue to network with them through email correspondence or social network presence and contact.

As I say this, it should be pointed out that the most effective way to network remains face-to-face interaction, but online contact offers another means to network.

The bottom line is that just because you are an introvert doesn't mean that you can be a successful networker. There are ways to work around your inhibitions and the awkwardness of meeting other people. And, as you become more proficient at networking, you'll become more comfortable with it. Hopefully, it can become something that is fun for you instead of something you dread.

Whether you are an introvert or an extravert, you can benefit from the power of a strong professional network. When done well, networking can be a great tool for finding a new job…or jobs throughout your career. There's no doubt that people who are "connected" are often the most successful. When you invest in relationships, whether personal or professional, your investment will be likely to pay dividends throughout your life or your career.

Chapter 5—Shameless Self-Promotion

Self-promotion is the act of promoting or publicizing oneself or one's activities, in an orchestrated or intentional way. It's important for you to promote yourself and your talents, especially when it concerns your job search. I've heard it said before, "If you don't pat yourself on the back, no one else is going to do that for you." This thought is particularly appropriate for self-promotion. You could be one of the most talented people in your profession, however if no one knows that, it's unlikely that you will ever benefit from your talents and expertise. If you want to ensure career success, you'll likely have to spend some time promoting yourself and telling others about your strengths, talents, and abilities.

Identify Your Strengths. Before you promote your strengths, you're going to have to determine what they are. How do I do that, you ask. One of the best ways to do this is to simply take a look at your past job descriptions and use those as a starting point for listing the responsibilities of those jobs. In doing this, you should highlight responsibilities you've had in previous jobs, paying particular attention to the tasks you really enjoyed in those jobs. Also, take a look at the tasks which came naturally to you in those jobs, the tasks that were easy for you to learn. These are likely to be things that will help you identify your strengths.

For example, a client of mine is a public relations professional. She has worked for three different companies in which she's been responsible for promoting the company or organizing various company-sponsored events. This woman loves organizing events and taking them from start to finish. That's been a favorite part of the public relations jobs she's had, and her past experiences with that help identify event planning as one of her major strengths. On the less tangible side, this woman is a tireless worker who will do whatever it takes to complete a project to meet the assigned deadline. This also counts as one of her major strengths.

Another way for you to determine your strengths is to look back at previous job reviews and find out what superiors identified as your strengths. Also, your current and previous colleagues should be able to help you determine your strengths. If possible, I suggest that you ask these colleagues what they perceive to be your strengths and talents.

Another way to identify your strengths is to look at the areas in which your colleagues search advice or help from you. If they keep coming to you for your help or advice in any particular area, chances are that they view that area as one of your strengths. And, in determining strengths, it's also important for you to identify the tasks or projects which energize you. Do you find that you lose track of time on any of the tasks you have had in your current or past jobs? If so, this may well be something that you enjoy, something that is a strength of yours. At worst, it's something you definitely might want to pursue in future jobs. Ideally, in promoting your strengths as you look for another job, you should concentrate on the things you enjoy about your profession, not the things you dislike.

In identifying your strengths, it's important to note that skill and passion are not always connected. For example, I was an A Honor Roll student in high school, but I never had much interest in academics. Also, I was an all-conference baseball player even though I never had much of a passion for that sport. On the other hand, I had a real passion for basketball, however I was never as good at basketball as I was at baseball, as I was "vertically-challenged" at basketball, having to continually play against players who were much taller than I was. So even though something may be a strength of yours, if it's not also a passion, you may not want to self-promote that talent as you might pigeonhole yourself into jobs you're good at, but don't enjoy doing.

Personal Branding Tips That Bring Employers to You. The goal of personal branding in conjunction with any job search is to differentiate you from other people who may be applying for the same jobs. As I've mentioned before, having just a resume and a cover letter probably isn't going to be enough to get you the job of your dreams. With this in mind, many people are developing their own personal brand to enhance their image as an industry expert, to detail and complement their professional image, and to secure the jobs or projects they're looking for.

Personal branding is much like corporate branding. It gives you a chance to take an active role in managing and promoting your own image, instead of depending on what others say about you. In establishing your own personal brand, you'll be able to tell prospective employers and recruiters about your strengths, talents, and qualifications. You'll be able to convey who you are and who you want to be.

Before you start to establish your own brand, you will have to first determine what you want to be known for. For example, the Wendy's restaurant chain is well-known for its hamburgers. Although it advertises and sells other items such as chicken sandwiches, French fries, and soft drinks, the chain knows that hamburger sales are the key component to its success. The same goes for you in your personal branding. Although you may have multiple talents and abilities, you'll need to define your primary talents and abilities. You'll need to determine who you are and what you want to be. You'll need to determine what motivates you and what you can bring to the table for a prospective employer.

Then you'll need to determine who your audience is and how you're going to reach them. In a previous chapter, I've discussed at length the importance of a LinkedIn profile for most people who are looking to land a professional job. I've seen research numbers that indicate that over 90% of recruiters utilize social media platforms to find professional job candidates; almost all of these recruiters are using LinkedIn as the prime social media platform. The exception might be for extremely visual jobs for which a portfolio will do a better job of explaining what you do or what you've done. Photographers, artists, graphic designers, interior designers, and other like professionals are likely to benefit from some of the portfolio web sites we've previously detailed. However, even with the portfolio web sites, LinkedIn is a platform which allows people to link to portfolios or web sites. And some people will want to expand on their LinkedIn presence with their own personal web sites, blogs, podcasts, etc. Anything you can do to give prospective employers or recruiters a better idea of who you are and what your talents are will enhance your chances to get the job of your dreams.

As you go to establish your own personal brand, I suggest that you familiarize yourself with how the leaders or experts in your industry brand themselves. Check out their web sites, blogs, podcasts, magazine articles, and see how they are promoting themselves. In doing this, you'll pick up some ideas or methods that you'll want to imitate. You'll also want to develop your own twist for your personal brand and determine how you can improve upon the ways these other industry leaders are promoting themselves.

Another way to establish your brand is by requesting informational interviews with industry leaders. You'll be surprised at how accessible various industry leaders are. You'll find that many industry leaders are generous with their time and most of them will be genuine in providing you with information that will help your career. For those of you who are not familiar with the concept of an informational interview, it is an informal conversation in which one person will sit down with another person with the goal of obtaining career information from that person. An informational interview is not a job interview. In most instances, the party being interviewed will not even have a job opening.

I'll give you an example. I have a friend who had a restaurant marketing job in his early 20s. His goal was to parlay his marketing job into a sports marketing job. As a restaurant marketing associate, my friend would travel all over the country. Whenever he got the chance, he would research the major corporations in the city he was visiting to see if they had sports marketing departments. And then he would call to see if he could set up an informational interview with a sports marketing person. He wasn't looking for a job per se; he was primarily looking for information on how to get into sports marketing. He had tremendous success with his approach and he was able to get informational interviews with some marketing vice presidents and marketing directors from companies that either had sports marketing departments or people who were marketers for professional or college sports teams. My friend asked the people he met with about the paths they took to get their particular job and he asked for recommendations on how he might go about getting into the sports marketing profession. Those informational interviews were non-threatening to the person who gave the interviews; they offered the chance for one person to help another in getting into the profession of sports marketing. It should be pointed out that even though my friend met personally with many of these sports marketers, that was a time before video conferencing such as Skype or FaceTime was available. With today's technology, it's even easier to use video conferencing for an informational interview. And if video conferencing isn't an option, a simple telephone interview can also be effective, although not as effective as face-to-face or video.

Another tip for you to use in branding yourself is to develop what is known as an "elevator pitch". For those of you not familiar with an elevator pitch, it is simply a 30- to 60-second description of what you do. Imagine that you meet someone you haven't met before on an elevator, and they ask you what you do. You have only 30 seconds to a minute to convey to them what you do before the elevator stops and either you or the party you're speaking to has to get off the elevator. The same concept works well with networking, where you may have limited time to explain to someone what you do.

An online presence is almost a necessity for you to build your own brand. Besides LinkedIn, many people now have their own personal web sites or web pages. Those same people often use other social platforms such as Facebook or Twitter to promote themselves. With your online presence, it's extremely important that you consider what kind of image you want to convey with your personal branding. Also, it's important for you to remain consistent with the image you portray over the different platforms.

And there's more to personal branding than just online branding. As discussed previously, things such as networking and participation in various professional organizations or associations also offer opportunities for you to build your personal brand.

A friend of mine owns a promotional products company which sells imprinted promotion items such as t-shirts, caps, coffee mugs, pens, just about anything on which a corporate logo could be printed on. As part of his personal branding, he developed a cartoon character he named Promoman. Promoman is a cute and memorable character who wears a superhero's cape with a big P on his chest. My friend features that character on all of his company promotional materials. This form of branding has been very effective in getting customers and prospective customers to remember my friend's company. Another friend of mine owns a handyman business that performs various residential repairs, primarily for people who are not good at fixing things around the house. He calls himself Handy Dan and uses that moniker to brand himself and his one-man company.

Establishing a personal brand is not a "one and done" proposition. You will need to continue to review and update your personal branding, just as companies and corporations are continuously modifying or adjusting their brands. I'd recommend that you review your online presence at least once a month, even if you have a job. In doing this, you'll ensure that your brand remains fresh and doesn't become outdated.

Less-Known Strategies for Self-Marketing. Although I've already outlined the best-known self-marketing techniques, there are some additional ways in which you can build your personal brand. Below, I've listed some different ways you can promote your brand. Almost all of these techniques offer you inexpensive ways for you to enhance your brand.

--Seek recognition for your expertise. If you're knowledgeable in any particular area, you should establish yourself as an expert in that niche. The friend of mine who is a promotional products salesperson entered an association contest in which he won an award for a campaign he did for one of his clients. He received an award from the association for the creativity exhibited in that marketing campaign and he immediately leveraged that award by sending out a press release to the local newspaper and by posting that news on his social media sites and his personal web site. In doing so, he was establishing himself as an expert in the promotional products industry.

--Share your wisdom. If you have valuable information to impart, share it with others. The same promotional products salesperson mentioned above promotes his brand by conducting seminars at the national association trade shows. He has also appeared as a guest speaker at some of those shows, conferences, and conventions. Although he rarely gets paid for his efforts, he uses these opportunities to establish himself as an expert in his field.

I have two other acquaintances who enhance their brands by offering to conduct an hour-long radio show in which people can call in to the station to get advice. One of these acquaintances is in the computer repair business and, on a show called "Tech Talk", he takes calls from people who are having computer problems or are seeking computer advice. In return for his non-paid services, the station allows him to promote his own company/brand throughout the show. The other acquaintance is an automobile mechanic and he does something very similar, hosting a show called "Car Talk" in which he fields calls every Saturday morning from radio listeners who are experiencing car problems or have car questions. I've also heard similar radio shows from financial planners, gardeners, lawyers, stock traders, and real estate agents.

Besides radio shows, you can share your wisdom and promote your brand by writing your own blog, by writing guest blogs for other web sites, by posting comments on other blogs, by teaching a community education course. One of my clients has a passion for major league baseball and he runs a site which highlights his favorite major league baseball team. One of the things he does to build his brand is that he gets on various major league baseball blogs or forums and offers his opinion regarding some of those blogs or topics. In doing so, he often works in the name of his own site. However, he is not blatant in doing that, as he doesn't want his comment or content to get flagged as spam. The same guy writes guest blogs for other major league baseball web sites. He writes these guest blogs for free in return for being able to mention his web site at the bottom of his blog. And finally, he also appears as a guest "expert" on various local radio shows, where he talks about his local major league baseball team.

   --Teach a class. Most communities or organizations sponsor classes in which people can become educated on various subjects. Again, most of these teaching gigs are non-paying gigs, however they'll allow you the opportunity to promote yourself as an expert in your field. My neighbor works for a bait and tackle store and he teaches a community adult education class on how to make your own fishing lures and flies. Another friend of mine teams up with a graphic designer friend to offer a community ed course on how to self-publish and market your own book. (The grapher designer instructs class attendees how to get an inexpensive cover design and how to format the book.) These two guys have also done this same course for some of the area libraries.

   --Podcasts. My sister and her husband create podcasts on parenting and they've convinced a local radio station and a local tv station to provide links to their podcasts. A local appliance repairman has developed and posted some YouTube video clips in which he tells people how to repair various household appliances. Obviously, he deals mostly with simple repair problems, but he is well aware that people with more complicated problems will turn to him whenever they themselves can't fix something.

   --Brand everything possible. Although no one would suggest that you have a tattoo of your brand on your forehead, you should be conscious of branding as many things as possible. If possible, place your name and personal letterhead on any correspondence you send out. The same goes for emails. If you are an accountant, instead of using a stock folder from the office supply store to hold a person's tax returns, you should make sure the folder is printed or contains a sticker with your own personal branding. If you are sending out a cover letter with your resume or a business proposal to prospective customers, or a thank you note to someone who granted you an interview, you should include your own personal brand whenever possible. The promotional products salesperson I've mentioned previously in this chapter even his a Promoman bobblehead character which he presents to customers who place orders of $1000 or more. This bobblehead character costs him less that $10 and offers him a way to keep his brand in front of his customer all year round.

--Keep in touch with your network. Birthday greetings, holiday greetings, thank you notes, and responding to posts on networking sites are all ways you can keep in front of your network. And don't limit you correspondence or self-marketing to professional contacts. Friends and family can also be a valuable part of your network.

--Be a community sponsor. Regardless of what community you live in or what online communities you participate in, most of those communities host events in which they are looking for sponsors or volunteers. These events offer you opportunities to promote your own brand. A friend of my wife has a side hustle gig in which she sells homemade salsa. She is trying to turn her side hustle into a full-time business. In an effort to build her brand, she often donates product to various organizations. For a local church festival, she donated salsa and chips for people to taste test at one of the festival booths. The people tasting her salsa could then register to win a year's supply of her salsa. In participating as a sponsor of the church festival, this woman was not only able to get lots of people to taste her product inexpensively, she was also able to build her brand inexpensively.

In summary, self-promotion is a mindset, an attitude. There are many different ways for you to build your own personal brand. Although you won't want to use all of the above self-promotion techniques, you should be able to use many of them in your attempts to establish yourself as an expert in your field and to create your own personal brand. And, best of all, with many of these techniques, you won't have to spend a lot of money to accomplish your goals. It's a simple matter of making yourself aware of the opportunities around you and then establishing a plan on how you're going to build your brand.

Chapter 6—Breaking Barriers

In providing you with tips and techniques on how to find a job, I realize that I might be a bit presumptuous in not pointing out that some of you might be fighting personal battles or inhibitions in searching for a job. Maybe you're sabotaging your own efforts to get a new job without even knowing it. Maybe you're someone who is prone to social anxiety or shyness and you find the thought of searching for a new job to be simply dreadful. Searching for a job, networking, creating an online portfolio, building a brand, and self-promoting...these are all activities that require the correct mindset and attitude. If you're not in the right mode of thinking regarding any of these tasks, you may be hindering your own chances of getting the job you want.

Four Ways You Might Be Sabotaging Your Own Job Search. Sometimes we inhibit our own efforts to getting a job, even without knowing that we are doing so. Here are a few common ways that people get in the way of their own efforts to get a job.

1) **You're using unrealistic language.** Some people make the mistake of using unrealistic language, especially in written correspondence such as cover letters. Over the years, I've had clients who have claimed to be "perfect fits" for the jobs they are applying for. Or they'll say in their cover letter, something like "I'm certain that you'll agree that I am highly qualified". With wording like this, you're not leaving any room for anything other than a yes or a no from the prospective employer. If I'm the person who is doing the hiring and I read a cover letter that says you are the "perfect fit" for the job I'm hiring for, my initial response is to say to myself, "Well, we'll

see about that." Or if you're telling me you're certain I'll agree with something, you basically telling me that you're taking away my role as the person doing the hiring. Yes, it's okay to display an air of confidence with your statements, but you're not likely to be successful if you are too brazen or cocky with the statements you make.

2) **You're applying for jobs that you're really not qualified for.** In determining which jobs you're going to apply for, it's important to set realistic goals. Yes, it's okay to dream big, but you'll have to be practical in determining your chances to get any given job, unless you want to waste your time or spin your wheels a lot during your job hunt. For example, if your current job is as an entry level marketing person, it's unlikely that you're going to be able to secure a vice president of marketing job for a major corporation. If you can be realistic in your expectations, you'll find that your job search will be much more efficient.

3) **You're highlighting skills that are not related to the job you're applying for**. If you have previous experience which centered around managing a large team of employees, but the job you're applying for does not include managing a team, then there's no reason to highlight that in your resume or your cover letter. It's okay to mention this experience if it is a major part of your work history, but don't place it near the top of your resume or highlight it in your cover letter. Or, if you speak Mandarin Chinese, but that has nothing to do with the job you're applying for, I wouldn't even mention it. In applying for any job, you should refer to the keywords in the job description or posting and then relate how your experience

or expertise fits with what the prospective employer is looking for. Many job applicants make the mistake of not adapting their resumes to the jobs they are applying for. Be flexible with your resume. If one of the keywords in the job posting is management experience, and if you have management experience even if it wasn't your most recent job, you should not hesitate to move that management experience closer to the top of your resume…and also mention that experience in your cover letter. Be flexible in adapting your resume to the job you're applying for.

4) **You're ignoring or trying to hide your lack of requirements.** If you ignore your lack of qualifications for any particular job, you should know that such a deficiency may well hurt your chances to get that job. If you're lacking some of the experience or the qualifications that the prospective employer has noted in their job description, but you are still very interested in applying for that job, it will be best to approach that deficiency head-on. For example, if the job description highlights that the employer is looking for an individual who has had management experience and you don't have management experience, you should address this in your cover letter, instead of simply ignoring it or trying to hide that fact that you're lacking in this experience. You might say something like this in your cover letter: "Your job posting mentioned that you would like to hire someone who has management experience. Although I don't have any previous experience in managing a group of employees, I have always received performance reviews that compliment me as someone who can lead when necessary and someone who works well with others." In doing this, you'll be explaining your lack of management experience and, at the same time, acknowledging that this is experience they are

looking for and then telling them that you don't expect that this will be an obstacle should you be hired for the job.

How to Overcome Social Anxiety and Shyness in Your Job Search. It's no secret that job hunting can be stressful. And it can even be more challenging if you are anxious or worried about the process. In my experience, there are two main things you should focus on in overcoming your anxiety.

First, it's important that you maintain a positive attitude throughout the process. If you're one of those people who tends to think negatively more than you think positively, you should make a constant effort to restrict your negative thoughts throughout your job hunting process. Try to turn your job hunting process into a positive experience instead of a negative experience. There's an old saying that is particularly applicable for this situation. "A problem is an opportunity waiting to happen." I suggest that you adopt that thought as your mantra throughout the job hunting process. If you can maintain a positive attitude throughout the process, you'll enjoy the process much more than you would if you let negative thoughts overwhelm you.

Second, in hunting for a job, you'll quickly find that whether or not you get a job is often beyond your control. You can't control whether a prospective employer offers you a job or not. With this in mind, it is important that you focus on the process of looking for a job instead of the outcome. I'm a big sports fan and I have heard numerous coaches tell their players to focus on the process, not the outcome. There are often huge discrepancies in the talents of many sports teams. A college football team that loses almost all of its games will have very little chance of beating a top ten team. So, coaches on the less talented team will often instruct their players to focus on the process, not the outcome. If a team works hard to try to become better, focusing on the process of doing that, they'll have a chance to get better and maybe someday they'll be able to compete with some of the much more talented teams. I recently heard a college football coach praising his team after they lost a game by the score of 56-7. "We worked hard all week and we limited our mistakes, but we just played a team that was bigger, stronger, and faster. If we can continue to work to get better week after week, I think we may be able to compete with them someday."

The same goes for job hunting. You may not be getting jobs because there are other applicants who have more experience than you. With a situation like that, it's important for you to stay positive and to focus on the process of getting a job, not the outcome. You can't change your history. If you're lacking in experience compared to other applicants, you can't change that. But if you can explain your lack of experience, someone is eventually going to give you a chance.

Here are some other tips and techniques to overcome anxiety you might have in searching for a job:

1) **Develop and implement a plan**. Maybe you're overwhelmed by how big of a project finding a job seems to be, especially at the outset of looking for a job. Most of us feel that way. The best way to minimize that problem is to come up with a step-by-step plan on how you're going to "attack" the process of hunting for a job. If you can divide the overwhelming task of looking for a job into a set

of smaller and more manageable tasks, the task of looking for a job will look a lot less daunting. You can take baby steps with this process, although you should assign a deadline to each of the projects so you can make sure you're moving forward and not procrastinating.

For example, maybe you just got laid off from your previous job. One of the first steps you'll want to take is to research the process of filing for unemployment. Subsequent tasks might include determining what kind of job(s) you want to apply for, creating a resume, developing or updating your online presence, researching job openings on some of the popular job sites, notifying your network of you impending job search, etc. If you can break down the complete task of looking for a job into individual projects like this, you'll find the process of looking for a job to be a lot easier and a lot less stressful. If you can do one or a couple tasks every day, you'll get closer to getting the job you want.

A friend of mine is a successful author who writes crime fiction books. He tells me the story that when he first decided he wanted to be an author, the thought of sitting down and writing a 500-page book was so overwhelming that he waited years to start writing his first book. He was able to do that only when he broke down all the tasks of writing a book into smaller, less daunting individual tasks, such as developing an outline, determining characters and the personalities of those characters, determining a setting and researching that setting, etc. After he did that, he resolved to write no less than 5000 words every day. (Other authors resolve to write one to three chapters every day.) His books average 90,000 to 100,000 words, so he knew that if he could produce 5000 words per day, he could complete a book in about 20 days. At the same time, he resolved write from 7 a.m. to 11 a.m. every day. (He prefers to write early in the morning so he then has time to spend with his family in the evenings. Other authors find that they are more productive in the evenings.)

You should take the same approach in your job search. I have many clients who resolve to spend a certain amount of time every day or every week looking for a job or preparing to look for a job. The time you spend looking for a job will obviously depend on whether you're currently employed or not. So, depending on how much time you have to look for a job, you should resolve to spend a certain amount of time every day or every week in looking for a job. Maybe it's five hours a day; maybe it's 20 hours a week. Some unemployed people even take the approach that looking for a job is their full-time job until they get one, so they'll work 40 to 60 hours a week at looking for a job. I have also had clients who resolve to apply for a specified number of jobs per week. Although most of these people understand that quality trumps quantity in any job search, they also understand that job hunting can be a bit of a numbers game and they know that the more jobs they apply for, the better chance they'll have of getting a job or at least an interview. A friend of mine who is a freelance writer has resolved to apply for a minimum of three writing projects every day. Sometimes, she gets multiple offers within a short period of time and she has to tell some prospective clients that she can't do their project immediately, but she finds it much easier to turn down a project than to have periods of time when she has no projects at all. In coming up with your plan to find a job, you'll have to figure out what works best for you, but I suggest that you come up with tangible goals and objectives to ensure that you're spending the right amount of time in looking for a job.

2) **Don't place all your eggs in one basket; don't count on a single opportunity.** I am always surprised at how many

people will wait until they have heard the outcome of one job application before they embark on another application. This is a major mistake, from a practical standpoint, an emotional standpoint, and a logistical standpoint. It doesn't make sense to let a situation control you when you can instead control the situation. Even if you've applied for your dream job, you have to remember that you're not the one who gets to decide whether you get the job or not. That lies with the prospective employer. With that in mind, you should make sure that you continue to move forward in your job search, applying for multiple jobs if possible. If you are fortunate enough to get multiple job offers from your applications, you'll be in an enviable position, able to choose the job you prefer. Remember that prospective employers are interviewing multiple candidates; there's no reason for you not to be exploring multiple opportunities at the same time.

3) **Look for jobs when you have jobs.** The best time for you to look for a job is when you have another job. It's a lot less stressful and you'll find that you're in a much better position in deciding whether or not to take a new job. This being said, I am always surprised at how people do not like to do this. As an example, a company in a neighboring community announced that it was closing one of its factories two years in advance of the closing. They did this with the idea that their employees would then have plenty of time to look for other employment. The company even offered classes and an allowance for employees to be trained in other professions. Yet, when the plant finally closed, only 37% of those employees had taken advantage of this extremely generous offer from the employer. In fairness, some of the employees who didn't take advantage

of the offer were near retirement age and they opted to take an early retirement. However, a majority of the employees there were going to wait until there current job expired before they embarked on a new job search. Unfortunately, this happens all too often with most people. You need to remember that it's much, much easier for you to look for a job if you already have another job. You have a lot more leverage and it's a lot less stressful. Even if you can allocate only a couple hours a week to searching for your next job, networking, updating your social media, or creating your brand, you'll be better off if you can do so while you're employed.

4) **Practice interviewing.** Before any interview, I strongly suggest that you prepare yourself. Research the company you're interviewing with; try to determine what interview questions you might be asked and determine what your answers will be to those questions. When I've interviewed for jobs, I've always conducted an internal dialog in which I imagine what questions might be asked of me and my responses to those questions. Other people will use friends, family, or colleagues for that process. Another way to get ahead of the interview game will be to research common interview questions on the internet. Anything you can do to practice for your interview should enhance your chances for success.

5) **Don't dwell on negative thoughts and scenarios.** Again, a positive mindset is extremely important in the job search process. It's important for you not to let negative thoughts overcome your positive thoughts. In applying for jobs, you're dealing with outcomes that you can't control, so the

goal should always be to focus on the process, do the best you can, and let the chips fall where they may. I have a friend of mine who is a pessimist by nature. He often imagines worst case scenarios instead of best case scenarios. He told me the story of an interview he had for his first job after he graduated from college. He was applying for a public relations job. For whatever reason, the prospective employer had all four of the people who were to be interviewed show up at around the same time. So, all four candidates were sitting together in the lobby. My pessimistic friend quickly determined that he was the only recent college grad among the four candidates. He also noticed that while he was wearing his off-the-rack interview suit, the other candidates seemed to have better clothes to wear for the interview, and instead of vinyl portfolios, they were carrying leather briefcases. Upon seeing this, my friend presumed that his die was cast; he'd have very little chance of competing with these other candidates. Ends up, he got the job. The woman who did the hiring later told him that she was open to someone who hadn't already established bad habits in another job; she liked the fact that he wasn't as polished as the other candidates, but had expressed a sincere interest in learning the ins and outs of the job and working hard. She also thought that his personality would be a better fit with the other people on the public relations team. The moral of the story: Don't let your negative thoughts control you, especially in a process you can't control. You never know why a prospective employer will hire one person over another. So, it's a waste of time to dwell on the reasons why someone won't hire you.

Job Search

6) **Consider hiring the services of a career coach or counselor.** If you have the budget to do so, many people benefit from the use of a career coach.

7) **Have an explanation for your social anxiety.** One of my clients suffers from extreme social anxiety. This affects him when he is speaking in front of large groups and it affects him during the one-on-one interview process. He and I talked extensively about how to solve this problem. He acknowledges that his anxiety is mostly related to a fear of failure. His social anxiety is so bad that he sweats profusely when he is placed in some social situations. Although I have never accompanied him to an interview, he has told me that, on occasion, he has experienced flop sweat similar to the sweat that actor Albert Brooks experienced as a television news broadcaster in the movie "Broadcast News". In the movie, Brooks' character was sweating like a running faucet as he did his first newscast. My friend tells me that he has had to have a handkerchief in hand before during interviews because he was sweating so much. He's also had shirts that have been soaking wet. So, for him, the way his anxiety manifests itself so severely that he's lost numerous job opportunities as a result. However, now whenever he goes on interviews, he is quick to explain his problem. He is quick to point out that he experiences anxiety in interview situations and tells them that "Some people don't think that I interview well because of the anxiety I have during the process. If you can get past my anxiety, you'll find that I will be a loyal, hardworking, and conscientious employee who will sincerely value the job opportunity you're offering." With this explanation, you'll note that he is facing his anxiety head-on instead of trying to hide it. His last two employers have been able to

get past his anxiety and have hired him despite this misgiving. I've had other clients who have also broached their social anxiety or shyness with prospective employees by saying, "I am a shy person, and I sometimes don't come across well in interview situations, however I can assure you that I will be a valued employee here. I may not have much style, but I can assure you that I have plenty of substance."

8) **Utilize a support system.** The job search process is often a difficult process and you'll certainly be able to take some of the anxiety out of that process by finding someone to talk to or to support you during this process. Many people who are looking for a job decide to make the process a solitary process and then they find that the process is depressing because they have no one to discuss their feelings with. Don't hesitate to ask family, friends, or colleagues to lend moral support during your job search. And, don't forget that almost all of us have gone through the job search process and it's not difficult to find someone who is familiar with the trials and tribulations of finding a job.

9)

Develop an Attitude that Attracts Success Now. Success is all about attitude and effort. You should know that success doesn't happen to you…it happens because of you. Success is something you have to earn. Most people don't automatically attract success. People attract success because they work hard to achieve it. They make sacrifices and they consistently strive to become a version of their better self.

Job Search

I've previously mentioned the mindset in which a person views problems as opportunities. This is extremely important for people who want to become more successful. People with the "problem is opportunity" mindset will find it much easier to inspire faith, confidence and trust in others.

People who are successful have the ability to "attack" problems instead of letting those problems control them. I'll give you an example. One of my clients was about to embark upon a job hunt. She asked me for my recommendations about how she should go about establishing an online presence that would enhance her chances of getting a great job. This woman was smart, but she wasn't technically-oriented. I was very surprised to find out that she has set up her own personal web site, created some podcasts, and created some blogs within just a short period of time. I asked her what her mindset was in creating her online presence and she said, "I viewed it as an opportunity to teach myself some new skills. I attacked these projects with a 'can do' attitude. I knew going in that there was information available on the internet on how to do each of those tasks, so I simply did my research and I learned how to do it." This is a woman who will attract success, because she is willing to do the necessary work to achieve it.

Another way to achieve success is to fail. Yes, you can achieve success by failing. There's an old saying, "When you fail, you learn. When you fail more than anyone else, you learn more than anyone else." Success is the direct result of the number of experiments you perform. If you're trying things and failing, you're likely to eventually be successful. On the other hand, a person who never tries is unlikely to ever succeed.

A few other tips on how you can start to attract success:

--Be authentic, genuine, and vulnerable. Don't be afraid to admit when you don't know something; don't be afraid to learn new things.

--Be a giver instead of a taker. Most people are takers. They'll take anything they can get, even if they don't need it. But you'll find that giving time and effort without expecting anything in return can be a key factor in positioning you for professional success.

--Shut up and listen. Always remember that you can learn a lot more by listening than you can learn by talking. So many people are intent upon showing other people how much they know that they often forget to listen what other people have to say.

Again, attracting success is all about attitude and effort. If you have the right mindset, if you're willing to give instead of receive, if you're willing to listen, if you're willing to learn and not afraid to fail, then you'll be a lot more likely to attract success.

Chapter 7—Job Interview Secrets

I doubt that I'll surprise anyone when I state that the interview is a critical part of the interview process. If you've ever lost a job opportunity because you didn't interview well, you'll be well aware of what a disappointment it is to get that far along in the job search process and then not get the job because you didn't make the impression you wanted to make. In this chapter, I'm going to give you some advice on how you can make the best possible impression in your interviews with prospective employers.

Golden Rules to Make an Excellent First Impression in a Job Interview. There are a lot of different things you can do to ensure that you have the best possible chance to get a job based on your interview.

--Make sure you're prepared. First of all, do your research. Research the company you are interviewing with by visiting their web site and by doing an internet search to find additional information on the company. Research the person you are interviewing with, checking for a LinkedIn profile, social media, and an internet search. Determine what kind of dress attire the company has and then select appropriate attire. If you're interviewing with a law firm, you're likely to dress different than you would if you were interviewing with an internet startup company. If you're not sure what would be appropriate attire, call the receptionist at the company you'll be interviewing with, tell them you have an upcoming interview, and ask them what the normal dress attire is there.

Make sure you know exactly how to get to the location where the interview will be conducted and then calculate the amount of time it's going to take to get there. (I've taken test drives before to determine how long it will take to reach an interview location. Don't forget to account for heavier traffic at different times of the day; likewise, don't forget to account for road construction on your route.) Being late for an interview will probably be a deal-breaker. Many years ago, when I was hiring for a small company I owned, I passed on a candidate simply because she was 10 minutes late. She apologized immediately when she arrived, telling me that her husband, who had delivered her to the interview, was running late. Immediately, I thought to myself that if the job wasn't important enough for her husband to get her to the interview in time, then that could present a problem in the future. Turns out that she was the best candidate and I liked her slightly better than the other candidates, however I ruled her out because she was late for her interview.

And, although you're probably already familiar with the job posting or the job description, make sure you review multiple times and remember the keywords from the posting. Highlight those keywords in your interview and make sure you explain any areas of expertise you have in those keyword areas.

--When you meet the person who will be interviewing you, make sure you greet them with a firm handshake (not a floppy fish handshake) and also make sure that you make solid eye contact with that person. This may not seem important to you, but this first 30 seconds of the interview process is very important to some interviewers. I'll confess that I will give bonus points to people I meet who have a firm handshake, eye contact, and a bright smile.

--Be observant. It's important that you are able to be aware of your surroundings and also the person you are interviewing with. If you're waiting for your interview in the lobby of a company, observe what's going on. You can tell a lot about the culture of a company just be seeing how employees interact with each other in the lobby. Also, how does the receptionist handle phone calls? If he or she treats each caller as if they are an interruption, that might be a sign that there's something wrong with the company culture. I once had a job interview for which I waited in the lobby for almost a half-hour, as I was early for my interview and the interviewer was conducting another interview. In the 30 minutes I spent in the lobby of this company, I determined that the company I was hoping to work for was probably not a good place to work. The receptionist wasn't all that friendly and almost all of the employees who came through the lobby had negative demeanors. So, use your time in the lobby to check out the corporate culture.

Along the same lines, you need to be able to read the person you're interviewing with as the interview transpires. Is the interviewer a serious person? Is their style formal or casual? Do they have a sense of humor? Are they truly interested in your answers to the questions they're asking or are they just moving down a checklist? Is the conversation flowing smoothly or is it a bit uncomfortable? Either way, you'll have to analyze what's happening as it happens, and then you may have to make adjustments accordingly to increase the comfort level of the interview or to find common ground. In finding common ground, I encourage you to look around the office of the interviewer if you get the chance. Most people have some personal effects displayed in their office. You might see things like family photos, bowling or golf trophies, framed diplomas or degrees, etc. If you can find common ground with any of these personal effects, use that information appropriately during the interview. For example, if you see a photo of the interviewer with her daughter and you have a daughter also, that might be something you can talk about, if there is an opening to do so. If you see a golf trophy and you're a golfer, you should see if you can find common ground with that. Although it's very unlikely that you'll get a good job because you are an avid golfer, if you can convey that common ground to your interviewer, he'll be more likely to remember you. Don't underrate "common ground" in connecting with a prospective employer.

--Don't babble; don't be curt; don't be afraid to tell brief stories as to why you're the right fit for the job. If the interviewer is interrupting you during your answers, that's probably a sign that you're babbling or your answers are too long. On the other hand, if the interviewer is pausing without talking after your answer, he or she is probably waiting for you to expand on your answer. And, remembering that an interview is meant for you to expand on your resume and cover letter, it's often advisable to tell a story or two as to why you are the best candidate for the job. However, with any stories you tell, make sure that you're not longwinded in doing so. If the interviewer wants you to tell them more, they'll let you know by asking additional questions related to your story.

--Be positive. Be enthusiastic. One of the most common mistakes people make in interviews is that they will spend a lot of time ripping their current job or employee. In doing this, the interviewer may well think that this is how you'll be talking about her or her company when you interview for your next job. It's OK to say what you don't like about your current job or the current company you work for, especially if you are asked about it, but I would strongly suggest that you show some decorum in doing so and that you don't dwell on these negatives throughout the interview. Always try to be enthusiastic and positive when discussing the job you are applying for.

--Assorted common sense tips. If you have previous work to show, bring samples of that work. For example, if you are a photographer or a graphic designer, you'll want to bring a portfolio of your work to the interview. If you're an advertising professional, you may want to bring photos or samples from an ad campaign you worked on. And, pay attention to the vessel or container you use to hold these samples or portfolio. I've had an interviewee bring in his portfolio in a grocery bag; I've had a lady dump out most of the contents of her huge handbag on the conference table as she looked for a photo to show me. (It looked like she was getting ready to host a garage sale.) Make sure you turn your phone off and put it away during the interview. And, if you're going to wear perfume or cologne, go light on it. Please remember that just about every office has someone who detests fragrances, even pleasant fragrances. Make sure you have the correct name of the person who is interviewing you and make a point to use that name at least occasionally throughout the interview. If you are interviewing with multiple people, get all the names, writing them down, if necessary. Using someone's name is one of the most basic ways you can use to establish a connection. And make sure, you use peoples' names when you depart the interview. That leaves a good impression. i.e.—"Josh, thanks for your time today. Mike and Joe, I enjoyed meeting you."

--Close out your interview; find out what the next step is. Don't leave an interview without thanking the interviewer for their time. And don't leave an interview without finding out what the next step is. When will they be making their decision? Will they call you or how will they inform you about the outcome of the interview? Is it OK for you to call them to follow up? If so, when can you call them?

--Follow up. Follow up immediately with a "thank you for the opportunity to interview note". I recommend a snail mail note that is handwritten if it's a short note or typed if it's a longer note. I discourage emails, as they can be too easily deleted. I prefer paper notes or thank you cards, because the recipient is likely to hang on to them for a while before disposing of them. And then in following up with phone calls, make sure you contact the interviewer when he or she told you to call them. And try to remain visible without becoming a nuisance.

Expert Tips to Stand Out in a Competitive Market. If you've reached the interview phase of a job search, you've already placed yourself above other candidates who did not get interviews. But now the going may get tougher as you compete against candidates who have been deemed to be more qualified than the others who have been left behind. There are still some things you can do to leverage your position as you head into your interview.

--Do your research. Just last week I had a human resources professional tell me how she views a person who has done his research going into an interview. "It's refreshing to meet with a candidate who knows what they're talking about and who has already researched the company. It's nice not to have to spend all of my interview time describing my company to the person I'm interviewing." The same human resources person told me that she also checks to see if the applicant has customized his resume and cover letter for the job he is applying for. "If they haven't taken the time to do that and they are using a generic resume and cover letter, I tend to think that they may not be all that interested in the job opportunity we have to offer."

--Provide links to your online brand. If you've cleaned up your online media presence (i.e.—your social networks), then it might be a good idea to provide links to your personal web site or portfolio, you're LinkedIn profile, your Facebook and Twitter pages (if appropriate), your blogs, your podcasts, or any articles on the internet which show you in a positive light. The person doing the hiring is likely to do this anyway, but in providing links to your information, you'll make their job easier and, more importantly, you'll be able to "control the narrative"/control the information the interviewer sees. I've had clients who provide this information a few days in advance of the interview through an email and that seems to work well for them. If the interviewer is going to do his or her homework before they interview you, you'll have made their job easier and you'll be able to control the narrative.

--Personality and attitude. In the interview itself, make sure you find a way to show your personality. It may surprise you, but many employers admit to hiring personality and attitude over experience. They're looking for someone who is going to be passionate and enthusiastic about working at their company. So, when you go into your interview, make sure you go in with a positive attitude and make sure you show your enthusiasm toward the job you're applying for. As another hiring manager once told me, "It's hard to fake an eager attitude. We always look to see how eager an applicant is about the job we're offering."

--Accomplishments and results over skills. Always concentrate on your accomplishments and results over your skills. Your skills are already listed on your resume. If you have specifics to show your accomplishments in previous job, be specific. The same goes for any results you've produced in previous jobs. Some examples: A brand manager instituted a brand campaign which increased the sales of a product by 11%; a football coach took a program that won two games the season he was hired to a program that won nine games only three years later; a management team professional took a department that had a 65% turnover rate to a department that had only 12% turnover in his tenure; a salesperson for a product line increased sales of that product by 32% within a year. The same goes for any accomplishments you may have achieved: Employee of the year in a company of 120 employees; won an industry award for a public relations campaign; president of a college chapter of professional journalists; editor of the college newspaper. You get the picture. In listing specific accomplishments, awards, and achievements, you'll be able to offer some tangible proof on why you're the right person for the job. This will allow the interviewer to put some specifics behind the skills you list on your resume.

The 10 Job Interview Questions You Should Always Know How to Answer. Whether you get the job you're looking for may well depend on how you handle or answer the questions that are asked of you. Although you can never be sure what questions you'll be asked, there are some standard questions that you should definitely be able to answer. And if you know you to answer these basic questions, you'll be much better prepared to answer any questions you might get. As a matter of fact, I would suggest that you use these basic questions in preparing for every job interview you have.

When I was fresh out of college, I lost a job opportunity because of the way I answered what should have been a simple question. The interview was going well until near the end of the interview when the hiring manager asked me "How my family members would describe me?" It was a simple question, but I totally blew it when I used the

"L" word. I told the interviewer that "My sister might say that I'm lazy". Yes, I referred to myself as lazy in an interview. I don't know why I said it and there was no truth to it, but I said it. When I said it, I knew immediately that I could stick a fork in my chances of getting the job I wanted. I tried to walk back my statement, but the die had already been cast. Although I don't expect you to botch a question like I did, I'm going to be quick to tell you that it is important for you to run through how you will answer questions in an interview before you have the interview.

Below I've listed some basic interview questions which you're likely to run into over the course of your interviewing career. Although I personally consider some of these questions to be mundane, the basic premise of these questions is for the interviewer to get to know you and to find out if you're a good fit for the job they are offering. The goal is simply to get you to talk and then the answers you give will possibly separate you from the other applicants, either positively or negatively.

1) **Can you tell me about yourself?** This is a very common question and I suggest that you definitely have a practiced elevator pitch in answering this question. In the period of a minute or two, you should be able to tell them who you are, emphasizing who you are professionally over who you are personally. And you should do so with confidence.

2) **Why do you want to work here?** This question provides you with a chance to show that you've done your research on the company you're interviewing with and the job you're interviewing for.

3) **How did you find out about this job?** If you have a personal connection, this is a good spot to use it.

4) **Why are you looking for another job when you already have one?** In answering this question, emphasize the positive aspects of the job you're interviewing for, not the negative aspects of your current job.

5) **Why should we hire you?** Here's your chance to tell what you can bring to the table and what places you above other applicants. Be specific whenever possible.

6) **Where do you see yourself in five years?** I'll admit that I detest this question, but it is one of the most frequently asked interview questions. If you have a specific plan, outline it briefly to the interviewer. If you don't know where you're going to be in five years, it's OK to say that you're not exactly sure what's going to happen, however you feel that this job will be a definite help in advancing your career path.

7) **Tell me about a conflict or disagreement you've had at work and how you handled that conflict?** This question is designed to determine how you can think on your feet and how you react to conflict. You should definitely have a prepared answer to this question, and always use an example in which you were able to resolve the problem with a satisfactory solution or compromise.

8) **What's your dream job?** Be honest in your assessment of what your dream job is, but hopefully include how the job you're applying for will help you get that dream job.

9) **What are your salary requirements?** Some employers ask this question; others don't. Either way, you should definitely know what your salary expectations are for any job you apply for.

10) **Do you have any questions?** Almost all interviews feature this question near the end of the interview. You should always have at least a couple of questions to ask in response to this question. Instead of saying that you don't have any questions or that the information the interviewer has provided has answered all of your questions, this "do you have any questions" question offers you the chance to show that you've been engaged in the interview process and a chance to stand out among other job candidates. Hopefully, you can develop questions as the interview has progressed. If not, you should go in with three to five questions to choose from and then select a question or two from that list. In asking questions, you should know that many interviewers enjoy this part of the interview, as it allows them a chance to deviate from the formal part of the interview and to talk about their company or themselves. So, the more relevant your questions are, the better chance you'll have to place yourself above other applicants.

Chapter 8—Make It Happen

Whether you are changing careers, negotiating a salary, or following up on your job application, here are some things to think about when you are doing so.

What You Need to Know if You're Changing Careers. Are you at that point in your career when you are ready to make a career change? If so, there are definitely some things you need to consider before making such a move.

Most importantly, I suggest that you plan for any career move. Some people make the mistake of jumping impulsively into a new career, possibly because they don't like their current career. That's a mistake that can increase the likelihood of failure in your new career. You should research thoroughly any new career or vocation you are about to embark upon. Find out what kind of education or training is required or recommended for this vocation. Research what kind of earnings you might expect from such a career. Review your current financial situation to make sure you have enough resources to subsidize a new career. Research the new career you desire by using the internet and by hopefully connecting with people who are already in that career. Informational interviews (discussed earlier) are in invaluable resource for learning about any new career you are interested in.

Job Search

If you have a spouse or significant other, are they on the same page with this possible career change? Certainly, any career change warrants multiple discussions with those people who are important to you.

In embarking on a new career, you should know that you may have to take a hit financially to get into a new career. If you are at a management level in your current career, you may have to start at an entry level or a lower level in a new career and this is likely to affect your income level. Do you have ways in which you can finance a new career? Maybe you will need to dip into your pension plan, your retirement savings plan, or your savings account. Maybe you will need to take out a second mortgage on your home. Or maybe you will need to take a part-time job to subsidize your new career, at least in the initial stages of the new career. Will you need to make any lifestyle changes to accommodate a new career? Longer hours? Less family time? More travel? If so, are these sacrifices you'll be willing to make? You should know that financial factors are the major reason people do not embark upon new careers. Financial strain, lack of financial planning, and debt can easily quash any career dreams or aspirations you might have.

Although you might be anxious to jump full throttle into a new career, I suggest that you consider whether you can get into that career in stages. For example, I have a close friend who was a corporate marketing executive for years. He'd spent a lot of time in a highly volatile industry where he was paid well but he found that he was a victim of layoffs frequently during these marketing stints. He was always a good and valued employee, but he was in a career in which there is a lot of turnover. Finally, he decided that he wanted a career in which he could control his own destiny. He also wanted the chance to get out from behind his desk in a job that was more tangible. His dream was to start a tree trimming and removal company. Yes, that's a major change from being a corporate marketing executive. Although he had helped trim and remove trees when he was younger, he really didn't know the ins and outs of that industry. He contacted various people who owned tree trimming companies, told them of his aspirations, and picked their brains on how he might go about getting into the industry. He was amazed at how helpful and forthcoming these other business owners were in telling him all about the plusses and minuses of the industry. As there aren't many classes teaching people how to trim and remove trees, he found an owner who allowed him to work as a paid apprentice on weekends while he continued with his marketing job. He did this for three months until he had enough knowledge to start his own company. He got his wife on board with his career move and she eventually became his scheduling coordinator and marketing person. Years later, he has a very successful career, with three different crews of employees who work for him in trimming and removing trees.

I did the same thing with a company I started many years ago. Instead of quitting my current job immediately, I hired a friend of mine who was between jobs and, based on my direction, she found an office location for me, priced out and purchased my office supplies and furniture, coordinated the development of my advertising and marketing materials, pre-interviewed secretarial candidates, etc.

In changing careers, you should also have a support system or a mentor that can either help you with your move or can be there as a sounding board. I strongly suggest that you enlist other people to help you as you make this career transition. It can be extremely difficult to embark on a new career, especially if you've been in another career for a while.

Job Search

If you can get your network or a mentor engaged in your transition, you'll have a much easier transition, especially emotionally.

Also, in changing careers, be prepared for setbacks. Always remember that things seldom go as planned. I've started two different companies that have experienced setbacks on two different sides of the spectrum. With one company, I'd had friends who had indicated that they would become clients of mine when I started my own company. But after I did start my company, I found that they were very slow to throw any business my way and that created a major financial strain to the point where I had to rent out my home and move into an apartment for a brief period of time. Finally, the people who had promised me business came around and my business flourished. I realized later that they were reluctant to give me business immediately after I started my company, as they wanted to wait and see if I was going to stay in business. On the other end of the spectrum, I started another business in which I had thought I had enough funds to finance the company for a period of six months, until I established the business. Three weeks into the start of my business, I received a huge order that I hadn't expected and I needed to use all of the funds I had saved for the venture to purchase products required to fill the order. And I needed more funds than I even had. Although it was a nice problem to have, it was a polarizing problem as I hadn't established a line of credit with a bank to finance the order. Thankfully, I was able to think outside the box and I got my customer to pay me in advance for the huge order in return for a discount on the merchandise. It should be pointed out that most companies would not have prepaid an order before the merchandise was delivered, as that wasn't a common industry practice. Bottom line was that I got very lucky with this order. So, in planning for a new career, you need to account for both worst case scenarios and best case scenarios.

And one more thought on changing careers: If you want to make a career change, but you're not sure what new career you want for yourself, you should be sure to evaluate the skills and the passions you've had in your past career. Take a look at the things you've done well or liked in your past career (also the things you have disliked) and use that information in determining a possible new career. Ideally, you'll be able to parlay some of your skills and passions into a new career. If you make a 180-degree change in careers and are not able to utilize some of your previous experience in your new career, your transition is going to be much more difficult.

Seven Negotiation Techniques to Get the Salary You Desire. After you've successfully moved past the initial interview stage and your prospective employer is ready to extend an offer, it's time to talk salary. Although some people liken the salary negotiation process to the negative experience of buying a car, you'll can't bypass this process in finalizing your job search. You'll want to make sure that you are getting a fair price for your services, regardless of what job you take. Here are some simple tips and techniques for you to use in determining what salary you deserve and then negotiating for that salary.

   1) **What is your market value?** It's important that you research what other people in your field are paid, both on a national and local level. You can consult salary guides on the internet. Or if you have a relationship with a recruiter, you might ask them what the salary ranges are for your career field. And always remember that where you're located will probably impact your salary, especially in regards to cost of living. A job in San Francisco or New York City is likely to pay more than the same job in a small town in Iowa, just because of the cost of living. Also, know what the market is for your particular job. If your prospective employer is having

difficulty hiring for the position your interested in, you have a lot more leverage than you do if it is easy for them to hire for that position. You should keep this in mind going into any salary negotiation.

2) **Don't say yes or no too early or too late.** Make sure you discuss salary before you take the job. If you take the job before you've reached a salary agreement, you've lost any leverage you might have in that regard. And if you delay in accepting an offer, the hiring manager might get frustrated and move to another candidate.

3) **It's not all about you.** Please remember that, in regards to your salary negotiation, your personal needs are going to have very little impact on the salary you are offered. A friend of mine who is a hiring manager recently had a prospective employee tell him that he required a specific salary so he could make his house payments and car payments. That's an absolute no-no. Your personal needs are not the concern of the hiring manager.

4) **Give a specific salary.** If a prospective employer asks you what salary you will expect or require in your new job, give them a specific salary or, at worst, a tight salary range. Don't tell someone that you want an annual salary of $60,000 to $90,000, as that's a very large range. If you offer a range, make it tighter. i.e.--$70,000 to $75,000. And remember that if you're giving a range, you're likely to get the salary on the lower end of the range you're requesting. And, one other thing, when an employer asks what salary you are expecting, act confidently without

being pushy. For example, you might respond as follows: "I've researched what other people in similar positions earn and, based on that, I was hoping for something in the $70,000 to $75,000 range. Is that possible?"

5) **Don't overlook the benefits.** Negotiating a compensation package often involves more than just salary. You should concern yourself with other compensation benefits and perks, which might include moving expenses, health insurance, vacation allocation, retirement savings plans, professional development opportunities, and advanced education benefits. With some of these benefits, the company you're interviewing with will have an established policy that they won't be willing to deviate from. i.e.—A company is not going to change its health insurance benefits because you don't like their current benefits. But, nevertheless, it's important for you to know what those health insurance benefits are. On the other hand, some companies do have flexibility with some compensation benefits, such as moving expenses, signing bonuses, and vacation time. If an employer doesn't have the flexibility to meet your salary requirements, maybe they have flexibilities in these other areas. If you are fortunate enough to have multiple job offers, you should obviously include benefits in your comparing these offers.

6) **Honesty is the best policy.** Don't inflate salaries from previous jobs. Don't make up competing job offers. If a prospective employer finds out that you've been dishonest, you're likely to become "history" with that employer.

7) **Get your offers in writing.** Once you and your future employer have agreed to a salary and a compensation package, make sure you request a written detail of that offer. That document should obviously be addressed to you and it should be signed by your employer. Unfortunately, I've heard of some instances in which an employer and an employee have a misunderstanding regarding salary and benefits and then the employee is often left at a disadvantage because he or she doesn't have written documentation of what was originally promised.

How to Follow Up on a Job Application the Right Way. If there is a job you're really interested in, you're probably going to be anxious to find out what's going on with the application you submitted. As a job applicant, you'll have to remember that, unlike the company doing the hiring, you're not in control of the process. This may be frustrating at times, but you should always remember that there are some right ways to follow up on your applications.

People often ask about what is the appropriate time frame to follow up after you've submitted your application. Normal time to follow up is about a week later. You can follow up in a number of ways, including phone, emails, or a LinkedIn message. If you are calling the company you're interested in working for, make sure you are prepared for what you're going to say, whether you speak to the hiring manager or whether you are leaving a voice message. Many people practice what they're going to say or will even have a few written notes on hand when they make the follow up phone call.

In following up, always be polite and professional. If you leave a bad impression, you'll likely be out of the running for the job before you even get an interview. Always make your messages brief, especially with phone calls. Appreciate the fact that peoples' time is valuable and they probably won't be interested in a long, rambling diatribe. That being said, there's no harm in including a sentence or two telling them why you are a good fit for their job offering. Anything that can place you above other candidates might well help you gain an interview. And, of course, with any correspondence you send, whether via voice mail or email, make sure to leave your name and phone number or email address.

Although it's OK to follow up multiple times, you should make sure you don't become a nuisance. And if you've tried multiple times to get a response without success, you may eventually have to concede to the idea that they're not interested in you.

Conclusion

If you've read this book, you now have the tools you'll need to get the job of your choosing. If you can follow the tips that apply to your job search, you'll be successful in your search...if not immediately, then eventually. In reading self-help books like this one, there are two types of people: those who will take the valuable information offered and implement it; those who will place this information on the back burner, saying they'll implement it when they get around to it...but then they never get around to it. I implore you not to be one of those people who never gets around to it.

You now know how important it is to "attack" what looks like the overwhelming task of finding a job into a set of smaller individual tasks that will make the process less overwhelming. You know how to find jobs that are advertised online and jobs that aren't. You know the importance of creating a killer resume, a cover letter that will place get your resume to the top of the application pile, and the importance of modifying your resume for each job you're applying for. You should understand the importance of having an online presence and a personal brand with a portfolio, a personal web page, blogs, and a LinkedIn profile.

Also, you should be well aware of the importance of networking and how to overcome the obstacles of networking if you are reluctant to do so. And you now know the importance of promoting yourself, establishing your own personal brand, and developing an attitude that attracts success. If you're shy or known to be afflicted by social

Job Search

anxiety, you should now have some tips at your fingertips to minimize those afflictions. You'll know how not to sabotage your efforts to get a job. You'll also know how to make a great first impression in an interview, standing out in a competitive market. And you now know what common questions you might expect during an interview. If you're changing careers, you now have some recommendations on how to turn that into a smooth transition. And you have tips on how to negotiate the salary you deserve in your new or current job. And you now know when and how to follow up on the applications you've sent to prospective employers.

Finding a great job is all about attitude and effort. If you can have a positive mindset and if you can do the work required to position yourself above other job candidates, you'll have a great chance to succeed in your job search.

Finding the job you desire can often be a lengthy or ongoing process and ultimately relies on decisions that are often beyond your control. But even though you can't control whether you get hired or not, you can control the process that allows you the best chance to get the job you're looking for. In order to be successful in your job search, you need to develop a plan and then work that plan.

As I've recommended multiple times in this book, in searching for a job you should always focus on the process, not the outcome. There may be times when you don't get the job you apply for, but don't let that discourage you. Focus on the process you're using to find the job, not on whether you get the job or not. You can control the process

Job Search

of your job search; you can't control the outcome. If you can do this, you'll have a great chance to get the job of your dreams.

Happy hunting!

STOP PROCRASTINATING

67 Proven Tactics To Beat Procrastination For Good. Get Things Done and Stop Your Bad Habits, Little-Known Life Hacks to Boost Your Productivity + Step-by-Step 30-Day Plan

Table of Contents

Introduction **115**
Chapter One: Beating Laziness **119**
    7 Tactics To Beat Laziness.. 120
    10 Essential Energy-Boosting Foods 123
    5 Tricks To Get Energized And Stay Energized 127
Chapter Two: Powering Up Productivity..................................... **129**
    Getting Things Done (GTD) 129
    Zen To Done Method (ZTD).. 130
    8 Productivity Apps You Need In Your Life Right Now 133
    12 Morning Routine Habits For Productivity 135
Chapter Three: Igniting Your Willpower **140**
    What to know about willpower? 140
    10 Powerful Strategies To Increase Willpower............................ 140
    12 Genius Tricks To Feel Instantly Motivated............................. 143
    15 Inspirational Quotes That Will Fire You Up......................... 148
Chapter Four: Your Daily Dose Of Self-Discipline **150**
    10 Expert Tips For Developing Strong Self-Discipline.............. 151
    7 Daily Practices To Keep Building Self-Discipline 155
    20 Positive Affirmations To Inspire Self-Discipline................... 158
Chapter Five: Finding Focus **160**
    10 Attention Exercises To Build Concentration 160

5 Mindfulness Exercises To Build Focus 162

10 Ways To Conquer Distractions.. 164

7 Foods That Can Help Boost Your Brainpower...................... 166

Chapter Six: Defeating Bad Habits... **169**

12 BAD HABITS THAT ARE KILLING YOUR PRODUCTIVITY 169

6 Ways To Eliminate Bad Habits Now...................................... 173

6 Ways To Create Great Habits That Stick................................ 177

Chapter Seven: Taming The Mind **180**

12 Essential Tips To Stop Overthinking And Control Your Mind 181

7 Techniques To Conquer The Fear Of Failure 184

6 Secrets For Creating A Success Mindset 186

Chapter 8: Planing For Your Success **189**

6 Techniques To Succeed At Goal Setting 189

5 Less-Known Goal-Setting Tips Straight From The Experts.... 191

7 Important Steps To Plan For Success 196

30 Day Step-By-Step Plan To Help You Build Habits And Fire Up Your Productivity.. **199**

Conclusion **210**

Introduction

Success and failure in life can be traced to one nurtured habit or the other. The things that make up your daily activities, the little mechanisms upon which your life runs, will ultimately determine how much you end up achieving. Habits build up into a daily routine, and these routines run our lives. All of these habits have been formed over time, through constant and dedicated practice. In this modern age, procrastination has become embedded into our DNA. The habit of procrastination has robbed most people of overwhelming success in life while enticing them with short-term feel-good rewards for just living the moment. Procrastination is a dream killer; a slow poison that dries up your zeal to achieve and leaves you wallowing in mediocrity. Procrastination is every promise you made to yourself but ended up breaking. Procrastination is when you let the goals you have slide due to lack of motivation. Procrastination is the roadblock that hindered you from reaching the place you had envisioned to be in five years ago.

Procrastination, even in its simplicity, is complex. Don't be deceived. In this book, I am going to unpack and dismantle the concept of procrastination. To enable you to tackle procrastination, you will need to understand the mechanism on which it works. Once the mechanism is fully understood, then techniques can be put in place to disrupt the mechanism. Throughout the chapters of this book, I will reveal to you various tricks and tactics used by the most productive people to overcome procrastination. I will be teaching you how to make good use of your willpower and stay motivated throughout the process. I only need you to believe that procrastination can be conquered and you will see yourself working to overcome it.

I am a self-help instructor with over five years of experience in helping people overcome the greatest hindrances to success. Through the

Stop Procrastination

years, I've noticed that the most subtle and dangerous obstacle has been procrastination. Clients walk up to me and complain about how they have put all success habits in place but have not achieved success. They seem to forget the place of time, which is a very crucial ingredient to success. Preparing for an exam a month before and two days before will not produce the same results. The reason for the latter is primarily due to a procrastinating mindset. This is why I decided to write the book to help people identify the bugs of procrastination clogging their lifestyle.

Now! Only a few people understand the power of that single word. Now encapsulates the present, the process of maximizing today. Everyday opportunities present themselves in deceptive manners. Some are quickly identified, and others would take the third eye to catch. However, catching these opportunities is one thing, maximizing them in that same instant they are found is another. Once procrastination is subdued, you instantly begin to reap the benefits in the now. Getting rid of procrastination is simply getting rid of weights that hold you back from acting when you know you should take action. Every opportunity seeping past you or ideas dangling in your head is tied to a deadline. Once the deadline is missed, the overwhelming success attached to that opportunity has been forfeited. And sometimes we won't ever come across such opportunities ever again. I am sure that sounds like that has once happened to you. Don't worry. You will learn to conquer it soon.

Each new day for me comes with a fresh testimony from somebody who has taken time to listen and apply some of the techniques I put into their hand. I receive calls from time to time from people who are glad they attended one seminar or another that I have given in the past. Their testimonies are wide-ranging and vast, covering a range of professions that had once proven to be stagnant before they were revived with the techniques I have been teaching. I discovered that the testimonies are somehow becoming overwhelming, and the testifiers were pressuring me to deliver more and more of my techniques. That is where the vision for this book came along. My main aim was to document as much as I could in one compilation so that these principles can go to places I might never be able to reach and continue the wonders they have been performing.

I have written this book in a simple style to so as not to alienate any of my readers. The techniques will be presented to you, the reader, in such a way that they can be easily followed and practiced. There are dozens of other titles out there that will only criticize you for procrastinating but will never provide you with enough information to counter your procrastination problem. There are little things that can be identified and worked on to give you the best experience while pursuing your goals. Did you know that a factor as negligible as dieting can affect how much you procrastinate? Of course, you will never hear that anywhere else. Just stick with me for this experience.

Some people have spent years procrastinating on the action to stop themselves from procrastination. In essence, they are just procrastinating on a miracle in their lives, the change that could take them to the next level. The great author, Paulo Coelho, said, "One day you will wake, and there won't be any more time to do the things you have always wanted to do. Do it now!" The subject of death is a sacred and greatly feared topic, yet it is so important. That said, you should keep in mind that every single day is drawing you closer to your death. If you don't start to change your life right now and get rid of procrastination, you will soon look back and have a trail of regrets following behind you.

I have heard people say that ideas rule the world. I beg to differ. In my opinion, it is ideas with the corresponding action that rules the world. Any life devoid of action is a life devoid of results, and what is a life worth living when there are no results to show for? Nothing in this book will be worth reading if you are not ready to apply the laid down principles that will be dished out to you. Your mind will continue to trick you into procrastinating on the change process, but it is up to you to conquer those mental roadblocks and take action. I will be stocking your arsenal with the weapons needed to bring down the enemy holding you back from reaching your full potential.

Chapter One: Beating Laziness

Laziness can go by different names at different times. Some refer to it as slothfulness, others call it idleness or a lackadaisical state of mind. But whatever the name is, we can all agree that laziness in any form is an undesirable trait that can rob you of success. Laziness is a state of mind, a psychological problem. You can refer to laziness as the unwillingness to use up stored energy. Or it can be said to be an unwillingness to undertake a task that you feel is difficult, boring, or time-consuming. Naturally human is laziness, and it takes an extra effort to overcome this innate nature and actually get things done. It is naturally easier to lie down all day long and get nothing done, to forfeit your goals and just watch time rush by. It seems like we humans are simply conditioned to live in mediocrity, to stay comfortable with anything that doesn't challenge our existence or survival. And this is the root of laziness, the foundation on which procrastination exists.

From a young age, the human body has always been bent on instant gratification. But truth be told, your dreams and aspirations will take time before they come to fruition. Allowing laziness become the order of the day will have you watching the seeds you have planted over time dry up before your face. Relating this to our present age, we seek people who absolutely live for nothing. Nothing inspires them, moves them to achieve more, or to do more to change their world. We see people who have accepted life simply for what it is. Technological advancements and changes in society has helped to facilitate the "Laziness Cause" even further. We now exist in a world where you can stay home all day and have everything brought to your doorsteps—your meals, your laundry, your groceries, etc. So, the question remains, "Why work, when everything can be done for you?"

Laziness and Your Goals

Of course, you can get comfortable with laziness and live the rest of your life bothering about nothing. Fact is, you will end up in mediocrity and with no tangible achievements to boast about. But if you are the kind of person that actually lives for something, that has a plan to outgrow their present level and become a success story that family and friends will want to identify with, then laziness is not an option.

One reason people are not motivated to work is that they can't see the beauty behind the achievement of long-term goals. Your laziness exists simply because you are uncomfortable with your present state. Once you make up your mind to leave your present state and enter the next phase of life, laziness begins to shake in its boots knowing that it is about to be knocked off. That is what you should do now. Don't procrastinate the elimination of laziness from your life. The more you postpone the action you need to take, the longer it takes before your dream come to fulfillment.

7 Tactics To Beat Laziness

Nobody likes being lazy. That is a funny truth. Most people who have discovered traits of laziness in their everyday life are not fully about the situation. The painful part is that figuring out what to do about laziness is hard. Think about your life at the moment: What are those things you would love to improve upon, ranging from family relationships, career prospects or financial status? All of these things are achievable; they can be improved upon to produce enviable results. There are tactics that can be implemented to help you overcome laziness in this regard and come out with overwhelming success. Let's study some of them:

1. **Have a clearly-defined strategy**

Laziness can't even be overcome if you haven't put down a strategy to go about achieving a particular goal. Say you want to get out of bed in the morning and achieve something for the day. You will need to have a list of actions set up for the day to help you identify where you should start with. In fact, having a well-structured strategy is already halfway to defeating laziness. The important question here will be: What is it that I want and how am I going to do it? Have a brainstorm session and identify ways of achieving your goals. Where do you need to go? Who do you need to talk to? How are you going to do one thing or the other? Write them down from the beginning of the process to the end. One thing you will notice as you put down your plans is that the joy of seeing them accomplished will come over you. That a step in the right direction.

2. **Be self-aware**

Laziness is a stealthy beast. You need know when it is around. Or maybe you know but you just can't do anything about it. One way to tackle laziness is the ability to identify what your laziness is. Laziness for you might be sitting through hundreds of Netflix movies all day and getting nothing done, but that is not laziness for a movie analyst or critic who gets paid to watch and rate movies. Other people can spend hours in a bathtub filled with bubbles and sipping red wine from a wine glass. That can be seen as relaxation, but at some point, it becomes outright laziness. Know how to identify when your relaxation has gradually slipped into laziness. Once you have been able to identify the presence of laziness, then it will be easier for you to fight it.

3. **Learn to love the things you do**

If you dislike an activity, the urge to do it will forever be missing. Sometimes, people aren't lazy, but they are not motivated to perform a certain task, and that results in "laziness." There are straight-A students who will procrastinate on writing their English essays because they hate writing, but they can spend hours and hours in calculus operations. Now these students not necessarily lazy, but writing essays is not something they enjoy. Although they might end up producing wonderful essays, the motivation to start was lacking, and this caused them to procrastinate.

Learning to appreciate whatever you need to do is a skill that needs to be developed over time. It might be a slow or gradual process, but in the end, it will surely pay off. Acquiring the right mindset will definitely have a drastic effect on how much you get done.

4. **Set a timeframe**

It could range from 10 minutes to one hour, and in this period tell yourself that there will be no break until you have carried out that task. You have thesis work to type? Sit behind your computer and type for the next ten minutes and see how far you can go with that. Set an alarm to gauge how much you can get done within that timeframe. Usually, your mind will immediately be conditioned to keep going after that task. In fact, your mind might become excited about the next challenge, seeing how much it has been able to accomplish within ten minutes. Once you get involved with the process, it is quite tempting to stop. After conquering the 10-minute challenge, you can then go further and keep pushing yourself. Go for a 30-minute benchmark and see how you fare. Then go for an hour, and so on. But remember that discipline is the key here. If you are failing at staying put for 10 minutes, there is a good chance that you will not succeed at 30 minutes. So, before you go any further, ensure that your body now understands what it means to sit and work for 10 minutes.

5. **Shut down any escape route for the time being**

What are those things that can constitute distractions for you and cause you to get lazy and procrastinate? Ask yourself: Where do I always escape to whenever I am not willing to work? Could it be a book, or a video game, or even Instagram? Whatever it is, it should be removed and taken far from you. Uninstall those apps if need be. Lock up those game pads in a drawer if need be. Do these things until you have achieved something worth achieving.

6. **Scold yourself**

When there is no one else to check on your excesses, you have to do that for yourself. When you no longer stay with your parents or someone older than you who can shout you out of bed, you should be able to do that for yourself. Remember that your body and mind are built to serve you, and they become quite dormant when allowed to do so. Get strict with your own self. You might call it discipline, but that word has been overused and has little value. Give yourself a talking to and say the things that you are scared to tell your own self. That way, your mind will understand that you aren't playing around anymore.

7. **See the benefits**

There is always something in store for you whenever you perform a task. Identify these benefits and brood over them. Take some time to appreciate them and see a future where they have all been accomplished successfully. Imagine the adventures you could possibly encounter by just beating laziness and taking that first step. Of course, there will be difficulties, obstacles and the like, but don't fixate on those. They will only discourage and help ruin the moment.

10 Essential Energy-Boosting Foods

A lot of people notice that they easily get tired, even after performing small activities at some point during the day. We have all been there at one point or another. It's 12 PM and you already notice that you can't drag your body off a chair. Your body suddenly become heavier. Taking in just any kind of food during this time does not help the situation. Keep in mind that food items that are high in fat and calories will leave you more fatigued than you were before eating them. They usually require more energy to digest.

Lack of energy can drastically affect your performance and your willingness to work. The truth is that the quantity and quality of food you eat can greatly affect your energy levels throughout the day. There are a variety of foods that are known to give energy, but only a handful of these contain the essential nutrients needed to increase the energy levels and keep you alert throughout the day. Foods like sugar or refined carbs can give quick jolts of energy that die within hours. But the body needs energy that is more sustainable, and this can only come from a well-planned diet. Work these following examples into your meals and see the wonder they will work in helping you combat laziness.

1. Brown Rice

This not the first food that might come to mind as per energy provision, but brown rice does wonders. Unlike white rice, brown rice is less processed and retains more nutritional value in the form of fiber. Brown rice is very rich in manganese, and it converts protein and carbs into fuel to energize the brain and body. This food released energy slowly and steadily throughout the day, helping to keep you motivated and alert. Brown rice can be served with vegetables to enhance its energy provision function.

2. Sweet Potatoes

Apart from their almost sugary taste, sweet potatoes are also very good energy boosters. They are very high in carbohydrates, beta-carotene (Vitamin A) and vitamin C which will keep fatigue at bay throughout the day. A small-sized sweet potato could contain about 22 grams of carbohydrates, 28% of the RDI (Reference Daily Intake) for manganese and an impressive 438% of the RDI for Vitamin A. The body digests sweet potatoes at a very slow pace thereby providing you with a steady supply of energy. Sweet potatoes can either be fried or boiled and taken with tomato sauce.

3. Bananas

Bananas are composed mostly of sugars such as glucose, fructose and sucrose. They also have some quantity of fiber in them. Bananas are a very good source of carbohydrates, potassium and vitamin B6, all known to provide the body with steady energy. Have a banana with peanut for a well-rounded snack, or throw slices of them into your morning cereal and watch yourself stay energized throughout the day.

4. Honey

A spoonful of honey is as powerful as half a cup full of energy drink. Honey usually acts as a time-released muscle fuel during exercise and it helps to replenish muscles after a workout session.

5. Eggs

A single egg contains about 70 calories in all, plus another 6 grams of proteins. Leucine, an amino acid present in eggs, helps cells take in more blood sugar, stimulate the production of energy in the cells and increase the breakdown of fat to produce energy. The energy released from an egg meal is provided very slowly for the body to utilize. Eggs are also very rich in B vitamins that help enzymes perform their roles in the food breakdown process. Eggs are also known to contain more nutrients in one calorie than most other foods. These nutrients can help to keep the hunger away for a long period of time. You can have your eggs scrambled, boiled, fried, or as an omelet.

6. Beans

Beans are very high in protein, and conventionally proteins are not believed to provide energy. But that is a wrong belief. Beans are a great source of energy, especially if you are a vegetarian. It contains a lot of fiber which slows down digestion. It is also rich in magnesium that directly supplies your cells with energy.

7. Coffee

Coffee provides you with that early morning jolt needed to get you alert and prepared for the day's activities. It works, and that is why a lot of people have a cup of coffee every morning to start their day.

Coffee is high in caffeine which passes quickly from your bloodstream over to your brain where it inhibits the activity of adenosine, a neurotransmitter that quiets the central nervous system. But it should not be abused. When taken in excess, it can get you jittery and interfere with your sleep.

8.   Dark Chocolate

This one rings strange, right? Let me explain. Dark chocolate contains more cocoa content than normal milk chocolate or any other form of chocolate. It contains antioxidants that assist in blood flow around the body thereby aiding the spread of energy. Because of this, oxygen is delivered more effectively to the brain and muscles. Also, the increased blood flow caused by these antioxidants also helps to reduce mental fatigue and help the mood.

9.   Avocados

They are highly rich in healthy fats and fiber. The fats help to facilitate blood fat levels and encourage the absorption of nutrients from the bloodstream. They are also stored up in the body and used up for energy when it is necessary. The fiber in avocados, which accounts for about 80% of the whole content, can help to maintain steady energy flow around the body. Avocados also contain a lot of B Vitamins which are required if the cell mitochondria will perform optimally.

10.   Nuts

Walnuts and almonds are noted to contain enough omega-3 and omega-6 fatty acids, and antioxidants which can increase energy levels and distribution in the bloodstream. Nuts have high calories, proteins, carbs and fats. All of these are nutrients that nuts release slowly throughout the day keeping you energized. Vitamins and minerals such as manganese, iron and vitamin E are some of the treasures that can be found in nuts. All of these give little jolts of energy in their own small ways.

5 Tricks To Get Energized And Stay Energized

Staying energized throughout the day is one sure way to get hold of laziness and prevent procrastination. The energy that is referred to here can be mental energy, physical energy or psychological energy. A deficiency in any of the following of them can cause a slowdown of the other bodily process. In our world today, it is commonplace to find out that you have totally become zapped of energy and you have lost your zest for life. Nothing breeds procrastination more than that. If you discover that you suddenly lack energy to carry on, then there are a lot of tricks you can use to snap out of it.

1. **Do something fun**

This one can help you deal with mental stress. The brain is a fun-loving sense organ that hates monotony and boredom. Once you have kept on with one task for so long and the brain gets tired performing the task, the zeal to return to it a second time and perform that task will never be there. Because the brain will dread that moment. Pause for a while and get your brain to do something different. Pick up your cat and stroke its fur. Play a little hide-and-seek with the dog. Listen to music while you work. Make sure you add a little fun to whatever it is you are doing, but you will want to make sure that you don't become distracted. After some time, you should get back to work.

2. **Take a short power nap**

Avoid the temptation to keep working and ignore the tiredness and stress. You are not a machine, and even machines themselves rest! Once you feel drowsiness coming over you, take out a few minutes and have some sleep. You can just bow your head on your table replenish your mind and alertness. If only you can understand the wonder of a short nap. It is like rebooting a system. Everything comes out new and refreshed, ready for a new phase.

3. **Go outside**

Get some sunlight and fresh air. Your body itself is always yearning for a new environment from time to time. If you have been in an office with air conditioning for hours at a time, it is time for you to go breathe some fresh air somewhere more natural. Walk to a park and watch the scenery. Observe the children playing with their pets and smile a little. Who knows, you might get inspired for next art project.

4. **Play mind games**

Get your brain and mind to work. Their dormancy might be the reason for your lack of energy. Do something that will challenge your mind, brain, and thought patterns. Read an article from the internet or a short story from a book. Play chess with your computer. Brainstorm with your colleagues. All of these things get your brain going and your body will instantly follow suit.

5. **Reduce your workload**

One major reason for fatigue and energy loss is size of workload. With a large workload you either get plenty things done badly or you get only a few done correctly. Streamline your daily activities so that stress can be controlled. Pay more attention to the most important activities. Then consider getting help from if you feel it is necessary.

Chapter Two: Powering Up Productivity

Productivity is the direct opposite of laziness. Once laziness has been successfully conquered, productivity comes next. Productivity requires a step-by-step approach for it to be achieved. It isn't just a one-off activity. That is why it is necessary to put systems in place to get things done when they should be done. This system will define your way of doing things, your methods, and processes. These systems can be developed, or they can be learned. In this chapter, I am going to reveal to you some systems that can help you get things done and become more productive.

Getting Things Done (GTD)

GTD is an effective way to organize and track your tasks and projects. The main aim of the GTD method of productivity is to ensure a 100% trust in a system for collecting tasks and ideas and plans. The GTD provides you with a way to track what you need to do per time and how you need to do it. Once the GTD system is in place, the amount of stress that you will go through trying to remember all the things that should be continuously done will be greatly reduced. Time is also saved in the long run. The GTD works by keeping lists with a paper and a pen. The main lists you will have to make with the GTD method include:

1. In
The In list contains all of your main ideas and action points as they occur to you. Just jot them down as they come to you and ensure that you miss not a single thing. You can use a notepad and a pen for this or an app on your phone. Just go with whatever works for you. What is important is that you miss nothing as they come.

2. Next Action

This list contains all of the possible actions you may want to take in the near future. From this list, you will pick out what you will need to do next when you are less busy.

3. Waiting For

The items on this list are those that have you anticipating for something to happen. Let's say you have assigned a task to someone and awaiting their reply. The waiting list is the perfect list to put that down. Write that down with a current date so you can keep track of the person's progress.

4. Projects

A project in this regard refers to any task that requires more than one action to get it done. All of these tasks should fall into your project lists. You can make it more interesting by writing down the details of each project so that it can be used as a guide.

On top of these lists, you might need a small calendar to keep track of time-sensitive tasks and events.

Zen To Done Method (ZTD)

The Zen to Done method was specifically developed by productivity strategist Leo Babauta to help individuals build habits in a step by step manner while working through a workflow management system. The ZTD teaches one to form one positive habit after another. It makes the whole process a lot easier when these things are tackled in this manner.

Stop Procrastination

Some people have found out that they perform better using the ZTD method over the GTD method. The key here is to find which of them works best for you. There are ten habits that should be adopted one at a time over the course of thirty days. Experiment with them until you notice changes in your habit pattern.

1. **Collect**

   Record your ideas into a book or a notepad. Write down ay tasks, ideas, or projects that may come to your mind at any point in time. This is different from the GTD style because the ZTD mandates you to carry a simpler tool such as a notebook or a stack of cards, which are easier to carry about.

2. **Process**

   Don't allow things to pile up and fuel your procrastination. Process your email, voicemails, etc. Put a decision on all of those items as you work: delete, delegate, file it, or do it later.

3. **Plan**

   Set out the things you wish to achieve each week. Ensure that each day is a step forward towards achieving that big project for the week. Be sure to achieve something daily.

4. **Do**

   Eliminate all distractions and get to it. Declutter your work desk and your mind so that you can have even more focus. With the distraction out of the way, set a timer and focus on the task for as long as possible. Don't try to multitask.

5. **Use streamlined lists and tools**

   Keep your lists as simple as possible. Don't allow the tools used in ZTD distract you from achieving productivity. Don't get caught struggling with the tools. Soon, you might find that the system has become too complicated for you to go on with it.

6. **Stay organized**
   Everything that belongs to you must belong to a space in your home. Once you are done using an item, it should be returned to that space. Create an organized system that works and helps you keep track of your items. Treat the organization habit like any other habit that should be developed and work towards developing it. Within 30 days there will be splendid results.

7. **Do a weekly review**
   Select a few of the long-term goals that you would love to focus on and accomplish with a space of six months to one year. Choosing many goals will only leave you overwhelmed without any tangible success. Break down a long-term goal into medium-term goals that will take a shorter time to accomplish. Create short-term weekly goals for each of these other goals. Each week, make a review of how far you have come in accomplishing that short-term goal during the week.

8. **Simplify**
   Your goals should be reduced to the essentials. Do a short review of all of your tasks and projects and find if you can simplify them. Even as you simply them, make sure that they align to the ultimate yearly goals so that you don't find yourself derailing slowly. Select only the stuff that matter.

9. **Set a routine and follow it**
   Build and develop routines that matter. Some these can include meditating, going for a walk each morning or reading at least a page each day. These routines can be developed for different times of the day, be it evening, morning, or afternoon. Also, develop a daily routine for different days of the week.

10. **Run with your passion**

    This last one is very important. If you are passionate about your work, the urge to procrastinate doing them will be greatly reduced or quenched totally. Constantly seek things that you are passionate about and pursue them for the greater good. If possible, make a career out of practicing them. Having such a list will give you the fulfillment that you crave as you accomplish each of those tasks and projects.

8 Productivity Apps You Need In Your Life Right Now

A productivity app is a software that makes your job easier and helps you gets things done in lesser. With the help of faster processors and wider connectivity, our smartphones have become some form of personal assistants to us. If you are aiming to improve your productivity level, some of the apps listed below should be at the top of your list. Each year, more and more of these apps are released, providing new and improved ways of staying on track of activities. Here are some of the essential apps that can boost productivity.

1. **ToDoList**

This app has been downloaded more than 7 million times from various app store platforms. All you need to do is pen down everything you need that you need to get done, and the app goes ahead to interpret and categorize all of your tasks based on the entries. The apps help you and your team stay on track while planning projects, discussing the details, and monitoring deadlines. The app goes for $36 per year for a premium version and $60 a year for full access to your entire team.

2. **TeamViewer**

This amazing app allows you access to all of your remote devices no matter where you are viewing them from. You can be in one place, and the app instantly connects to the files you need that is currently located somewhere else. The connection also goes as far as giving you the leverage to hold audio meetings, video chats, and file-sharing options. With all of these features, collaboration with a wider variety of people becomes easier, and things get done faster. The app is available for iOS users and Android users.

3. Yelling Mom

Yelling Mom is a fun app to use. It works on the principles of a nagging mother who won't allow you breathing space until you have done what she told you to do. Once you schedule a task, the app goes to remind you about the task before the deadline is over by making use of some annoying alerts like a wailing siren or a referee's whistle.

4. Serene

Serene is designed specifically to handle distractions and help you give more concentration to the things that need to be achieved for that day. The app is currently in a private beta stage, and you will need an invite to be able to use it. But it is worth keeping an eye on for the meantime.

Once you have set up your goal for the day, you will be required to break them down into smaller sessions which will last about 30 to 60 minutes each. Set a timeframe that will be long enough to complete the goal. Once a session starts, the app blocks out any app that might turn out to be a distraction. A countdown appears on the screen while you work, and there is an option to play soothing music as you work.

5. Coach.me

Coach.me is a platform that connects you with online coaches who will help you achieve your goals. You will find different coaches who are specialists in different categories you can choose from. The coaching is done by email, and it is beautiful because you get to meet somebody and make a friend as you change your habits. The coaches will reply to any questions you have.

6. Loop

Loop is an Android-only app, and it employs a rather different approach to helping you concentrate on tasks. Loop is a habit-building app. Instead of getting you away from bad habits, it helps you form new and beneficial ones. Whatever it is that you should invest more time doing, Loop will help you to do it. The major features of this app include

- setting a target for things that you invest more time doing
- Provide a score for how well you are performing in developing new habits
- Set reminders to energize you when laziness sets in

7. HelloSign

HelloSign takes away the trouble involved in signing a large number of documents by giving an option to sign them electronically. All documents that are signed through this app are legally binding because the signature remains real and not electronically engineered. An extra benefit is that all documents signed through the app are all organized so that you don't have to waste time sorting through them whenever you may need them.

8. Drafts

Note-taking and journaling just became easier with the Drafts app. Once a new entry is made, the app quickly tags them and sorts them out. You can use some of the tools in the app to convert your notes to emails, tweets, emails, or documents.

12 Morning Routine Habits For Productivity

A good morning always results in a good day. And your morning routine seems to really be a major factor that sets the tone for the rest of the day. The success of your day is dependent on the very little details of your morning. You have to understand yourself and the way in which your body works to be able to grasp the full potential of your morning routine fully.

Morning routines have been proven to help some of the most successful people on the planet to achieve their goals. Once productivity is missed in the morning, it is always hard to capture at any other point during the day. Here, we will study some simple morning routine that will help you boost your productivity during the day.

1. **Wake up naturally**

For one person, 4 AM the perfect time to wake up and start up the day. For another person, a perfect day starts up at 6 AM. The 6 AM person isn't necessarily for waking up some hours later. Take your time to get up from the bed. I am not preaching laziness here, but there are some times that the body itself still needs to gather itself out of bed. Forcing out of bed is one sure way to create chaos. The most important thing is to get your body in tune. Some people function better during nighttime, and they end getting up late from the bed. They have been productive for that day at least. Only make sure that your body stays alert when it is time for it to produce. Resting your mind and brain long in bed is better than staying out of bed and nodding off throughout the process. You will get nothing done right that way.

2. **Don't make major decisions in the morning**

It is better that you spend the evening before writing down ideas and preparing for the next day. The willpower to make good choices and decisions is greatly reduced in the morning, and it can slow down your brain from performing at an optimum level. Once you have your day all planned out form the night before, it will help your mind to immediately get settled and get to work on the day's activities.

3. **Start your day with exercise**

You might have heard this about a thousand times, but the importance of exercise to your body cannot be overemphasized. Your body is begging you to train it and let off some steam. People who exercise first thing during a workday are generally known to possess more energy for the day than others. You don't have to visit a gym. You can walk to the train station, skip a hundred times, or do something else that stretches your body.

4. **Clean and declutter your workspace**

An uncluttered workspace will give you more concentration and productivity. Once everything is disorganized, your ability to perform optimally is reduced. People who work in a clean and organized environment are generally more productive than others who are comfortable with clutter. Clutter takes your time because your work items will be easily misplaced.

5. **Complete the hardest and most tedious tasks in the morning**

One beautiful thing about the morning is that your mind is as clear as possible. Your internal environment is serene and ready to perform for the day. You should prioritize this opportunity and get things down, especially those things that matter to you. Settle all of those things before your emails start jumping in, and the calls start coming. Once you clear off those tasks, the rest of the day will go on more smoothly.

6. **Have a glass of cold water**

Hydration helps to bring your body alive. For the whole of the time you slept, your body stayed with freshwater entering the system. Once you take water into your system, it gets your muscles going and provides your body with new energy for the day. One of the biggest indicators of low energy is a dehydrated body. Start your morning refreshed by taking a full glass of pure cold water and observe the wonders it will do for your body.

7. **Reduce your screen time**

Except if you make your money online or you are an online personality that needs to keep fans updated in real time, then you should keep your phone out of reach in the mornings. Smartphones and social media have been revealed to be some of the biggest killers of productivity and facilitators of procrastination. You can decide to leave your phone in its drawer until lunchtime or put it into airplane mode.

8. Meditate

Meditation will help you tackle stress and anxiety emanating from the previous day. It is best done in the early morning when the world around you is quiet, and your mind is peaceful. Meditation helps you focus your concentration and complete one task at a time, instead of getting pulled over to different tasks. It enables you to stay present in the moment.

9. Streamline your decisions

The morning time comes with a lot of choices: what to wear, where to go, who to call, what to cook, etc. Work on these decisions so that they don't too much of your time each morning and cause you 'decision fatigue.' Have a routine for your morning, such as what to wear and what to eat. Make it simple so that the decision is made quickly and you can go on with your life.

10. Be grateful

Wake up each morning and acknowledge the good things in your life, no matter how small they may be. Take some minutes and practice gratitude. The process is rewarding, and it will provide you with a clearer vision for the day. It will also help you conquer negativity which is one of the hindrances to creativity and productivity.

11. Read a page or two

While exercise sets your body in motion, reading sets your mind into action. People who read are likely to stay ahead of those who do not read. Reading keeps you updated on the latest opportunities available to you and how you can maximize them.

12. Spend time with family

No matter how small it is, this is necessary. Talk to your kids. Laugh with your spouse and get them prepared for the day. A person who leaves home happy is more likely to participate better at work. The genuine happiness from know that joy exists in your family is enough to energize you for the day.

Chapter Three: Igniting Your Willpower

What to know about willpower?

Willpower is the ability to be able to control yourself; but it also goes just beyond ability as it sounds. It is a combination of will and power. Having to do something regular, relaxed, and pleasurable may not task your willpower. Often, your willpower is relaxed in the face of accessible decisions and tasks. The firm determination to do things that are difficult (such as wanting to lose weight or quit drinking alcohol) is the true definition of willpower.

Research has it that a part of your brain (the pre-frontal cortex) powers your willpower just like love and fear is being controlled by the limbic system of the temporal lobe. Willpower feeds on mental energy just like the emotions do, and this can cause you to be tired or fatigued.

I'm sure you can relate to what happens after jogging in the morning for a long time or after doing some push-ups to stay fit. Your muscles become naturally weak then. The same also applies to willpower when the part of the brain that controls it is stressed.

10 Powerful Strategies To Increase Willpower

I am about to reveal to you winning rules and tactics to help you hush up the voices that rise against your willpower.

1. Who are you?
'Man, know thyself' is a famous utterance by the philosopher Socrates. It is of the truth that you alone can tell your high and low points. There are limits to which your abilities can be stretched. You know at what points a joke becomes offensive to you.

Wanting to know yourself could bring you to ask some questions like;

Stop Procrastination

- How far can I go?
- How well can I do?
- Where am I most productive?
- When and where does laziness flourish in me?

2. Self-exploration

Many a time, you face a lot of restraining factors. Most likely, you hear yourself more often than you can count make statements like "I can't go beyond here; I wasn't made for this; I can't do this anymore." The moment the "NOT" word takes center stage in most of your activities, then, you should know that your willpower is on the decline.

Go explore your abilities, push yourself to do unfamiliar feats, and challenge the status quo. In simple terms, push the limits.

3. Stand your ground

"Tomorrow, I will increase my number of sit-ups by ten." "I will start drinking just one bottle of Coke per day from next week." "I will go an extra 200 meters at the next road walk." These are probably things you said but never did. Procrastination is a huge red flag in the path of increasing willpower. The moment you stop saying and start doing is the moment you will begin to record remarkable changes. If you don't stand your ground, the statements will become a popular future recurring rhyme. So, whatever you want to do, start Now!

4. Involve your imagination

Many inventions you find today are as a result of imagination. Someone imagined having to fly in the air as a faster and more convenient mean of transportation rather than drive on the road, and it came to reality. Today, we have the most sophisticated airplanes. Same happens with willpower. The body responds to imaginations just the same way it does to experiences. If you imagined that you fail a test, you would discover that you will begin to feel uneasy, especially if you are the kind of person who detests failing. If you are having a stressed day and you imagine yourself by a pool lying in a recliner with a bottle of chill drink and the feeling of cool breeze, your body will begin to assume that position and feel relaxed. Your body feeds on your imagination. Use the power of imagination to increase your willpower.

5. Learn to say NO

Most of the challenges faced by your willpower arise from your inabilities to say no to numerous pleasures that come your way. You tend to indulge yourself in too many activities that result into nothing.

6. Have a recovery strategy

If you want to succeed in increasing your willpower, especially on a long-term basis, then you will need to consider this. Fatigue can also apply to willpower. You may find it rather hard to sustain your willpower if you go on and on so hard without any break or space to recover. It's just a matter of time before you get tired and ultimately fall back to the start. Take some short recovery breaks.

7. Be conscious of your environment

Pressure and circumstance are vital to increasing your willpower. If you want to achieve or carry out a particular task, make sure you surround yourself with related things or people. If you want to maintain stable mental health, you may as well want to hang around people who are non-toxic and not volatile with whom you can have meaningful and positive conversations. Purge your environment of people and things that tend to want to soften your willpower.

8. Do it in bits

Willpower can drown in the presence of huge tasks. It is natural to get discouraged at the sight of heavy responsibility. It could even overwhelm you. Why not break it into bits? It is more comfortable and less challenging. Deciding to read a 1000-page book a day can prove to be daunting. However, dividing the book into parts and deciding to read some pages over a specific period feels easier to accomplish.

9. Set realistic timelines

Even though you are set to increase your willpower, going overboard is not encouraged. Setting unrealistic goals is like "building your castles in the sky."

How do you keep it simple?

- Add a little more time to your reading hours
- Do five more push-ups
- Read one extra book in 2 weeks
- Doing a few more will help you record little but vital progress.

10. **Understand that it is all up to you**

Your decision to power up your willpower is yours. You are not in a race with anyone but yourself. Make up your mind to do this for you.

12 Genius Tricks To Feel Instantly Motivated

Motivation comes in different forms. It could come like a spark of flame (within seconds or minutes) or gradually like a highly viscous liquid (in hours or days). The good news is that you can ignite any of the two mentioned. For this particular part, here are tips on how to get motivated almost instantly.

1. **Eat dopamine-releasing diet**

Dopamine is a chemical released by nerve cells and is usually associated with the brain's pleasure and reward system. The release of dopamine in your body creates a feeling of pleasure which motivates you to repeat a pattern of behavior. It means that eating foods that induce the release of dopamine can increase your motivation.

Nonetheless, bear in mind that some diets are capable of reducing the release of dopamine which could cause a reduction in motivation—foods like animal fat, butter, palm oil, and coconut oil fall in this category. It is difficult to avoid these foods altogether, but you can try to reduce their intake significantly. Employ your willpower to achieve this.

2. Take a more motivating posture

In emotional intelligence (EI), mainly when dealing with empathy, nonverbal communication is critical. It is because many important things are left unsaid that being able to figure the unspoken is crucial. The same applies to motivation. Some stances, postures, and body movements can influence your confidence. In other words, it can increase or decrease motivation.

- **Sit with your chest pushed out (don't slouch)**

Sitting with your chest pushed out (a confident stance) helps you to hold your thoughts with more confidence. Alternatively, if you sit in a slouchy position or with your back curved out, it is perceived as a doubtful posture and would portray a lack of confidence.

Recent studies have shown that sitting slumped in a chair can make one feel less proud of their performance. It can also lead to people giving up quickly on demanding cognitive tasks. So, sit upright.

- **Stand straight with "arms akimbo."**

Standing at "arms akimbo" means standing with the hands placed on each hip in such a way that the elbow flairs out. It translates into taking an expansive posture, which makes the body appear more formidable and taking up more space.

It shows dominance and confidence. The scientific explanation behind this posture is that it boosts testosterone (confidence hormone) and decreases cortisol (stress hormone).

3. Make positive pronouncements.

"I am making an exponential success," "I can do this because I was made for it," "Nothing can stop my success," "I have what it takes." Saying these things to yourself can greatly motivate you at any time and get you to perform better. Speak to yourself aloud.

4. Make a deal

When I say the deal, I mean tell a friend about your decision and request him/her to monitor you daily to ensure you are recording improvements. Make it more practical by adding a monetary commitment to the deal.

How do I mean?

Hand over some cash to your friend on conditions that if you can achieve your motivational goal, the money will be returned to you, if not, it should be donated to the charity.

5. Use the power of positivity to stay motivated

As long as you live, there would always be moments when negativity would set in. Sometimes, your entire day may seem to go wrong. Everything, for whatever reason, would decide to go south. Your boss at work chooses to frustrate every effort you make. Your kids could unexpectedly fall ill. Your colleagues at work appear to irritate you.

The stark truth is that we can't always control circumstances we find ourselves in, but it is our choice how we respond to them. You may find yourself in hard or unpleasant situations. Nonetheless, you will need to decide to stay motivated through them.

Here are some tips on how positivity can help you stay motivated.

- **Surround yourself with positive people**

It is said that "show me your friend, and I will tell you who you are" or you must have heard that "birds of a feather flock together." This implies that your circle of friends or association is an excellent determinant of who you are and how much you can achieve.

On the one hand, if you have around you people who are positive-minded or always optimistic even when it is hard to do so, you will most likely be influenced by their positive vibes. On the other hand, if you have a toxic or pessimistic association, you are bound to stay negative most of the time.

- **Don't dwell on things you can't control.**

There is indeed no perfect condition. Situations that are beyond your control are bound to come up. It is essential to be able to differentiate between things that are within and outside your control, rather than dwell on them or fret over them. If not, you will unnecessarily waste time on them and most likely become stunted.

6. Have a plan (write it out)

Do you set out for the day's activity without any ideas on how you intend your day to go? How eventually does it turn out? Do you take time to develop a schedule or plan on how you want your week to run?

It is no news that "he who fails to plan, plans to fail."

Making a plan is like having a road map to help you navigate your way into your activity for a period. It gives you a sense of direction. It also helps you cut short the time spent doing nothing or irrelevant things as well as help you enhances your productivity.

Having a plan makes you organized and gives you an inner feeling of satisfaction, especially when you can follow up on your ideas.

- Let's see how you can set up your schedule or plan for a week
- Create a list of activities you wish to carry out for the week
- Narrow the program down to a daily to-do-list
- Allocate a time range to accomplish each task
- Follow upon each task
- Check every assignment as you complete them.

7. Count your blessings and appreciate your little achievements

Once you can appreciate your little or significant achievements, you will stay motivated to achieve more. It is also important to know that forming the habit of positive reinforcement could be of great help.

Positive reinforcement is rewarding yourself for successes made or achievements recorded. For instance, after a long week of work and having achieved you set goals, you could decide to take yourself out on a treat. Buying yourself something you do not regularly buy or going to places of relaxation and recreation are good examples.

8. See from a new perspective.

If you have always had negative thoughts or feelings, you could decide to try out a new perspective of being positive. Being positive can alter your life in many ways than you can count. It is also incredibly interesting and exciting to take a positive form.

9. Try it differently

Having to repeat a routine could be tiring if it is something that would last for an extended period. Why not try it differently? Snap out of the routine. Seeing a situation or task from a different or new perspective could be quite adventurous.

10. Subscribe to motivational shows and speeches

Listening to motivational talks or reading motivational material can serve as a motivation booster. We are mostly a product of what we hear and read.

11. Go on an enjoyable and fun activity.

Sometimes, you could feel fatigued or worn out from doing the same thing over and over again. To stay motivated, you can engage in some activities that are fun and relaxing.

You could decide to listen to your favorite songs on your way to work, and you could also decide to take some time out during your break at work to stroll around. The feeling of being out of confinement is refreshing.

During the weekends, you can decide to exercise. Exercises have a way of releasing dopamine, which increases motivation.

12.   Talk to someone

Sometimes, you may fail while trying to motivate yourself even after working so hard to stay positive and motivated. It is ok when you get to this point. Do not beat yourself. Instead, talk to someone you trust. It could be a family member, or you could reach out to a counselor. He/she could guide you on the best approach to return you to motivation.

15 Inspirational Quotes That Will Fire You Up

There are a thousand and one quotes that can shoot you into being motivated to do things you never thought you could. Here are some of the thought-provoking and soul-lifting quote carefully selected.

1. "If you don't build your dream, someone else will hire you to help them build theirs." —Dhirubhai Ambani
2. "Don't beg the status quo, challenge it"- Anyanwu Emmanuel
3. "Whatever the mind of man can conceive and believe, it can achieve." — Napoleon Hill
4. "Great minds discuss ideas; average minds discuss events; small minds discuss people." — Eleanor Roosevelt
5. "Have no fear of perfection – you'll never reach it." — Salvador Dalí
6. "I've failed over and over and over again in my life, and that is why I succeed." — Michael Jordan
7. "Success is most often achieved by those who don't know that failure is inevitable." — Coco Chanel
8. "Our greatest glory is not in never falling, but in rising every time, we fall." — Confucius
9. "Life is 10% what happens to me and 90% of how I react to it." — Charles Swindoll

10. "The mind is everything. What you think you become." — Buddha

11. "Start where you are. Use what you have. Do what you can." — Arthur Ashe

12. "The secret of success is to do the common things uncommonly well." — John D. Rockefeller

13. "It is hard to fail, but it is worse never to have tried to succeed." — Theodore Roosevelt

14. "Success is not final; failure is not fatal: it is the courage to continue that counts." — Winston Churchill

15. "It had long since come to my attention that people of accomplishment rarely sat back and let things happen to them. They went out and happened to things." — Leonardo da Vinci

Chapter Four: Your Daily Dose Of Self-Discipline

Our world today has literally compelled us to some realities. And the convincing truth about this change is appalling. Think of success as one. To be successful in any job, you must have as an essential ingredient the technical skills to perform effectively. The added spice for excellence is creativity. But not everybody falls into this category. It is not because of anything; it is just that humans have not been able to set goals to achieve this. Setting goals gives you control. There is always a direction to go. It gives you an understanding of where you should start, which turns to take, and finally, your destination is secured. Some even have an idea of setting big targets, but get stuck along the process of achieving those long-term objectives.

There are different ways of achieving goals. Maintaining some goals (which may be a career, life, family, etc.) has on its strategies. This process depends on the person involved since everybody is not on the same level of achievement. Top management level personnel will have concise goals and will be very much useful in achieving it because of many years of setting goals. The experience involved will distinguish the success rate when compared to a lower management level officer.

However, with intense self-discipline, you are sure to maintain these goals effectively. Self-discipline is an essential and useful skill everyone should possess. And as important as this skill is, only a few people acknowledge its importance. Being self-disciplined does not necessarily mean you have to be too hard on yourself or express the same feeling to people around you. It does not mean you should limit your lifestyle to a boring one. The totality of self-discipline is having self-control. It is the ability to measure your inner strength and how it can be transformed to control your actions. You then have a consciousness to react without bias.

Having self-discipline enables you to carry on in decision-making, which helps you accomplish goals with ease. It is more of the inner strength to keep you going. It has control over other inner-core terrible habits. Addiction and procrastination is a deeply rooted habit which self-mastery will help eliminate. That said, it is evident that having self-discipline is necessary for our everyday life.

10 Expert Tips For Developing Strong Self-Discipline

The superb thing about self-discipline is that it is a behavior that can be learned. Our decisions are void of impulses and unsteady feelings. Here are useful tips for developing strong self-discipline.

1. Put A Date On It

Research has shown that putting dates on your activities helps you stay focused and determined to achieve them. It also helps in maintaining a regimen, which, in the long run, helps build strong self-discipline. For instance, you may attach an activity to Mondays, and consistently follow up with it. With enough time, you would have created a regimen for that activity and, in turn, have groomed self-discipline to always perform that activity on Mondays. You might think of fixing Thursdays for your karate class. Once you are committed for the first few weeks, a subconscious knowing will erupt. Even without setting reminders, you get to know that Thursdays is not for a pool party. Get a sticker and fix it on your calendar with the name of the activity. Or you can create a reminder on your mobile devices

2. Identify What Motivates You

Priority is essential in identifying how far you would be self-disciplined. Focus on the most important thing. There is no need to dabble into what will demean and destabilize you. And commitment would not set in if you are unsure of what exactly you need to do. There is always a high possibility of success when there is a feeling of urgency. Clothe yourself with "I must" mentality. "I must always look neat, regardless of how tired I get."

You need motivation to get started. Once you have prioritized your goals, attach modules that keep you going. Your goal might be to get a stable income to maintain a comfortable daily lifestyle. This goal is appropriate and specific. Once you identify that a steady income is essential, it will help you focus on your goals. With this realized, you can control yourself against other things that might have a negative effect on your income. Understand also that you can't be self-disciplined if you are not motivated to continue.

3. Affirm your goals and visualize the benefits you would gain

There should be a plan to achieve your set targets. Most times, we get distracted by the result that we neglect the strategies to make them work.

Analyze how you think this will work well for you. Make sure you are specific as much as possible. Outlined benefits will give you a sense of accountability. Imagine you have highlighted that one of the benefits of eating healthy is good body shape. The moment you start feeding well, and you notice the change in your body, you could quickly tick the benefits as the one you have achieved already. It will push you to a place where you will embrace other interests you have discovered.

Consistently affirm your goals and the benefits you would gain from them. Your mind will repeatedly get in tune with those set targets. If you say every morning, "I am a great athlete because I'll break the record to get a $4,000 scholarship," "I am getting that contract, and it makes me a better engineer." With time, your mind becomes disciplined and determined to achieve these goals.

4. Make Achievable Plans And Stick To Them

Temptations are bound to arise whenever you are determined to achieve a goal. It might be a distraction from social networks or even your friends. Some might also come when it seems you are not making progress. You will understand that this could hinder you from actualizing your targets. However, your goals must be attainable. Don't be ambiguous. Let it be profound to your taste, work condition, lifestyle, and routine. Include precise quantity, time, people, and dates. These variables make it easy to stick to your laid-down formula.

5. Make Your Regimen A Combination Of Things You Need To Do And Things You Want To Do

Management science research has shown that combining these two activities helps form good habits and also helps you quickly achieve the needed. You can get things done, even in the fun of doing other things. Just decide on what can be combined to give you the desired result. For instance, you want to have a girl's day out to talk and have fun. You can choose the same day you have set out for the gym. After some teasing, agree with your friends to go for a workout session. You can even make it competitive. That way, you have achieved an activity you need by combining it with an event you want.

6. Sleep And Eat Well

Lack of proper sleep and food causes the prefrontal cortex (which is responsible for self-regulation) to perform less than expected. Additionally, the ability for a person to focus when they are hungry reduces to the minimum as lack of food causes lack of sugar, which in turn weakens a person. Hunger brings in a sensation of unwillingness. It is always accompanied by tiredness. Your willpower to do anything is being affected. Thus, you are not motivated to concentrate on what you need to do. To stay focused and disciplined, make sure you eat and sleep properly.

7. Reward Every Progress

Do you remember when you were a child and your parents said they would reward you with a gift if you passed your exams? And whenever you pass, and they fulfill their promise, it is always a source of motivation for you to study more? This logic also works for building self-discipline. If you reward yourself for every progress you make, that way you stay motivated to do more, keeping your eyes on the benefits to be gained.

8. Get A Self-Disciplined Circle

External motivation is the first propeller of habit formation. Just as peer pressure can cause a person to form bad habits, having a circle of self-disciplined friends could motivate you to be self-disciplined. Just as the saying goes, "show me your friend, and I would tell you who you are." Put yourself around people who give you a sense of fulfillment. These are people who have the same belief system as you. Even when it seems you are losing willpower, you get to find strength in their resilience. You would get easily encouraged if you found out that your friends have been able to ensure mastery over a particular course you are struggling with.

9. Do It For Yourself

Self-discipline is good, but most importantly, it is best if the purpose is not biased. If you are aiming at getting more disciplined, be sure it is solely a decision made for you. That way, you would appreciate every progress you make. It doesn't mean that you can't seek professional advice or instructions from friends. It just means that you have to be truthful about your action plans without any form of prejudice.

10. Project Future Challenges

You wouldn't want to fall into self-deceit by believing that everything will work as planned. You might stumble, find out what triggered it, and resist falling into the same pit in the future. Forecast other challenges that might arise as you go on the journey of self-discipline. Think of distractions and problems. They don't have to subdue you. Create a plan to tackle it.

7 Daily Practices To Keep Building Self-Discipline

Self-discipline cannot be attained in a day. It requires consistency and perseverance, and daily practices can only build this. Commit yourself to know that the journey to maximum self-discipline is not a palatable one, but the end is always a meal to remember. Here are the daily practices you can use in building your self-discipline.

1. The Cold Bath Test

Everyone hates a cold bath, especially in the morning. That icy blast hitting your face when you are still trying to keep your eyes open can be pretty annoying. It requires a lot of resolution and discipline to subject yourself to that icy blast every morning. And if you can pull through it each morning, that is another step to maximum self-discipline. Prepare your mind for the fact that self-discipline wouldn't look appealing at the start. And it may even become burdensome and time-consuming as time progresses. It will require you a lot of patience and commitment, especially if it is not within your culture. But in the end, you will have more reasons to stay disciplined.

2. Daily Meditation

Sitting at a spot with your eyes closed and just listening to your breathing might appear dumb at first. But do you know that meditation is a great way to build self-mastery? Because it requires a high level of concentration for you to sit at a spot and consciously listen to your breath? Consider doing this practice every day, and you will increase the strength of self-discipline. Additionally, meditation helps clear your mind, which in turn enables you to reconnect with your inner self. Try sitting and listening to your breath every morning. After some weeks, you would have disciplined your mind to focus on your inner self and would have built your self-discipline through this exercise.

3. Identify Your Weaknesses

Every human being has weaknesses, and most of us tend to overlook them. Being disciplined means you understand your flaws, challenges, and weaknesses, yet are determined to overcome them. If you are a "glutton" but are committed to stop eating out of proportion, the first step is to acknowledge your problem. "Is it that I like to taste everything I see, or I don't get satisfied when I eat more of carbohydrates" Then, ask yourself, "how can I solve this problem?" Having acquired a solution, consciously follow up on it by having in mind the picture of the result (less weight). Admitting these flaws is the first step to overcoming them. Hence, to attain the maximum state of self-discipline, you must acknowledge that there is a need for it and the hindrances stopping you from achieving it.

4. Run Every Morning

A one-mile sprint takes about six to ten minutes and a new determination to pull through. It might appear hard to accomplish at first, but it is a useful tool for building endurance and discipline. Sprinting every morning gives you an automatic jump start for the day and enough energy to pull through it. Be sure you do it before the cold bath in other to maximize your self-discipline growth. If you are reluctant to do this alone, speak to a friend about it and both of you can get started. Ensure that your aim of running is fulfilled.

5. Make Your Bed

Everyone wants to wake up and jump off their beds and get on with their day. No one sees the need to take about two to three minutes to make their beds. Hence, it requires a lot of discipline to consciously decide to make your bed. Always convince yourself that it is necessary to fix your bed because it promotes a positive habit of neatness. The good thing is that it takes very little time. A conscious effort to do it every morning can improve your self-discipline significantly.

6. Eliminate Temptations

Temptations and distractions kill discipline. Without them, attaining maximum self-discipline is possible. However, their presence causes you to either be sluggish or give up. Every distraction or temptation is unique to each goal, and understanding them helps you eliminate them and stay on course, thereby building your self-confidence. Whenever you are tempted or discouraged, remind yourself that, "this is the best time to give my best."

Affirmations by itself will not eradicate temptations. Analyze those things that get you obsessed. Clear them and refuse to go alongside that direction. If you are trying to read, stay away from the PlayStation. Video games will not help you focus during exams. Make a schedule of when to hang out with friends if you see yourself wasting a productive moment with a close acquaintance. If you are having trouble studying an e-book on your phone because of updates of an adventure game, force close the app or uninstall it if necessary.

Let temptation be a positive reminder that you have been doing well, and this time is not the moment to give up.

7. Be Intentional About Your Goals

Getting an all-around commitment to daily targets is necessary for achieving more excellent results. You wouldn't be the best version of yourself when you have not been purposeful about your goals. Start by making it clear. Write them down. Your journal or notepad can be an excellent place to pen it down. You can as well write down any affirmations you think will motivate you to keep going.

20 Positive Affirmations To Inspire Self-Discipline

Whatever you say consistently to yourself sticks in your mind permanently. It creates a consciousness in which you work in. This is why assertions are a significant part of building self-discipline. Every day when you wake up, say these affirmations to yourself.

1. I am a fantastic person, and I am thankful for this opportunity to grow.

2. I am determined to make myself better mentally, spiritually and emotionally.

3. I must work on myself. I am doing the right thing.

4. This day is an excellent day for me, and I am going through it with a spirit of gratitude.

5. I adjust to who I am becoming: my strength motivates me, and my weaknesses are a discouragement to me. I overcome every fault. My shortcomings are turned to advantages.

6. On this day, I am intentionally defining boundaries and eliminating every form of distraction and temptation.

7. I have complete control of my time, and today I am not engaging in any bad habit.

8. I am strong and capable of becoming self-disciplined. And I would attain my maximum state of self-discipline

9. At every point in time, I know what I am expected to do, and that is what I would do.

10. I am accomplishing every task I have today. I am conscious of the benefits of living healthy. Therefore, I am guided to eat right.

11. I am giving my best at everything I do today. I prosper at the work of my hands.

12. Today, as I decide to do my daily routine, I achieve all that is set before me. I am organized and prompt in every area of my life.

13. No challenge can pull me down. I surmount every difficulty. Natural circumstances do not move me.

14. Worry will not solve my problems. Therefore, I will not be anxious about anything.

15. My imagination is active. I use my imaginative power to create excellence. My mind is open to receive new ideas. I am quick to act on positive impulse. I am motivated from within. Nothing can stop me!

16. My mind is attracted to positivity. I do not see negativity. I am making progress with giant strides.

17. I affirm that I am an advantage in my world. This is not the time to give up on myself. I am not ordinary. I am undaunted by challenges

18. I reign in life. All things work together for my good. I am strengthened and energized for victory today.

19. I am life-conscious. My body is energetic and full of vitality. There is no space for sickness, disease, infirmity, or anything that brings pain to my body.

20. Nothing can pull me down. I do not see the present temptation. I am full of benefits.

Chapter Five: Finding Focus

The average human has a short attention span that doesn't even last a mere eight minutes. Surprisingly, that is the attention span of a goldfish. Because of your digital life, this number has shrunk even further. The brain is always on the lookout for the next exciting thing happening in the environment. We are most likely to get bored because of this.

Your ability to focus and pay attention to your environment is essential to your survival. It is a skill, and you have to improve it to make it better. Focus is just like the muscular system of the body. The more it is exercised, the stronger and more substantial it becomes. The process of focus building is a mental battle that you have to partake in to better your self. Don't dwell on the idea that you are the kind of person who easily loses focus. Buying into that narrative will spell doom for you.

The question now remains, how can focus be built and developed? In an age where everything is vying for your attention and pulling you in different directions, what can be done to keep your mind at alert?

10 Attention Exercises To Build Concentration

As I mentioned before, your mind and concentration strength can be exercised to increase the value. Just like a gym instructor will dish out exercises for you to do to develop different parts of your muscular system, there are some other exercises for the mind that can be used to build your "concentration system." Remember, your success mostly depends on how well you can concentrate and capture the details that surround you. Here are some of those exercises you can do.

1. **Exercise One:** Take a book or magazine and open it to any page you may find interesting. Read up that page and understand its content. Begin to count the words on the page, one paragraph after another. As you count, take note of each word contained in each paragraph. Try to understand their function in each sentence. Then go over and make a recount.

Once you notice that you can easily count the words in the first paragraph, you can move over to the next.

2. **Exercise Two:** Count the numbers backward from 100 to 1. Make a picture of each number as you count and do this as fast as you can. Concentrate your mind on picturing the whole numbers in a line of ten. Increase your count to a range of 500 and 1000.

3. **Exercise Three:** Take an object and focus the whole of your mind on it. It could be a fruit, a toy, or any other object. Observe its components and features, the things that make up this particular object. Take note of its shape, color, size, flaws, and all. Continue to pick out all of these things and don't allow your mind to wander while you do this. Even if it does, bring back to base. Do this for three minutes at a time and continue to increase until you finally master it.

4. **Exercise Four:** The next time will be to visualize the object you have just observed. Close your eyes for a while and try to picture what you have studied for some time. How go does your mind bring back the image to you? Try to bring back all of those things that you discovered while observing the object. If your mind fails to produce a clear model, open it up for a while and observe again. Then close your eyes and see how well the image forms. Do this repeatedly until you are finally able to picture the object in its full form.

5. **Exercise Five:** Choose a particular word or phrase in your mind and keep repeating it to yourself in your mind. Do this silently without causing any attention towards yourself. Do this until your mind learns to concentrate throughout the process for about ten minutes.

6. **Exercise Six:** You can play a small game with your nose. When going through a flower garden or the local park, keep your nose open and ready to grasp the different types of flower smell that can be detected. This exercise requires some level of concentration to differentiate the various scents in the environment.

7. **Exercise Seven:** Take a good position and stay quiet. You can either lie down flat or sit on a chair. Do not move as you remain in that position. Keep your full concentration on your

heartbeat. Try to picture the mechanism of blood flow throughout your system and try to figure out where the blood reaches around your body. With constant practice, you will soon be able to feel your blood flowing through your body.
8. **Exercise Eight:** Practice the art of self-control. You might be the kind of person with a strong desire to talk and spill secrets about others. By learning to control these urges, you will be able to energize your concentration strength. To continually put these things behind your mind and force them to remind there is so much power than you can understand. It will help you put your will and desire in check. No matter how exciting the news may be, try your possible best to keep it under wraps until the appointed time for which it should be revealed.
9. **Exercise Nine:** Try to keep your mind void of any form of thought. This is probably going to be the hardest of all the other activities. Your mind is constantly being bombarded with ideas, and to keep them out requires a lot of concentration. Try to do this for one minute at a time. Once you conquer that timeframe, you can go on to five minutes and then ten minutes.
10. **Exercise Ten:** Engage in art. Art here does not only refer to painting, drawings, or sculptures. Art is a whole lot wider than that. Art is in your everyday conversation. Art is in the movies you watch and the song you listen to. Pay closer attention, and don't just do these things because you are bored. You might not know what you can discover, and you will ultimately learn concentration by paying attention to these little things.

5 Mindfulness Exercises To Build Focus

Focus is considered an essential ingredient to success in life or any endeavor. Focus is a rudiment to the improvements of your thinking mechanisms such as your learning ability, perception strength, and problem-solving. Learning to build focus becomes very important when these factors are considered. Focus helps you achieve mental clarity. There are several ways with which you can start practicing how to create focus and use it to complete any given task.

Mindfulness in this regard refers to a state of being present in the moment. It is being aware and open at the moment. Mindfulness deters your mind from wandering around and losing its place.

1. **Exercise One:** You are never your best whenever you are in a hurry. When you slow down, you learn to reconnect with the environment. Slow down as you walk through the driveway. Don't chew your food too fast. Take your mind and appreciate the world around you. Slowing down does not mean that you are sluggish or a sloth, slowing down is looking deeper and preventing mistakes. Remember what they say: Slow and steady wins the race.
2. **Exercise Two:** What do you see when you close your eyes. What lies behind your closed eyelids? The eyes are a major source of distraction to the mind. Close your eyes and cut away that distraction. Close your eyes and focus on the pictures in your mind. Listen to the sounds around you. Your other senses perform better once your eyes are close, so close them and see what you can discover.
3. **Exercise Three:** Train your eyes to catch the footprints pattern. Learning footsteps is one right way to understand human and animal nature. Footsteps are like messages that need to be deciphered. If you can train your mind and eyes to catch things as small and seemingly insignificant as footstep pattern, it will be quite easier to pick the essentials.
4. **Exercise Four:** Every time we are prone to emotions which we may not necessarily understand. We might soon find ourselves not paying attention to what we feel. This exercise involves you finding a name for your emotion and pinpointing the reason why you feel that way.
5. **Exercise Five:** Observe the people around you. You can practice in an office or in any public space. Keep your eyes on one person and note what they are doing. Observe their body language and their dress pattern. Try to keep a picture of them in your mind, so that forget them once you take your eyes away. Become more mindful of the people around you and the actions they carry out.

10 Ways To Conquer Distractions

Most of the time, we start with good intentions of having our minds on the task at hand, but something happens are we soon discover that we have lost focus. You know that you have the ability, the strength, and the drive to carry on, but distractions always have the upper hand and soon you notice that you have been overpowered. Think of distractions as small pests in your workplace that bore holes and prevent productivity. If you do nothing about them, they grow stronger and continue to build their net over you. If only you can take some time off and try to calculate how many hours you have lost to distractions, you will understand how bad the situation has become. And the truth is that distractions are so powerful, and conscious efforts needs to be made to be able to conquer them. Some of these strategies will help you stay on top and overcome distractions:

1. **Identify your sources of distraction:** Different people have different things that distract them. For some, it would be watching ballet dance videos on YouTube, while for others, it would be their own thoughts. All you need to do first is to identify what constitutes a distraction to you. This is the first step to take to eliminate these pests.
2. **Develop distraction-proof habits:** There are small habits built over time that can help you become a better person overall. For these habits to grow, first you must create a friendly environment devoid of distraction for them. It is never an easy task, and it will require a lot of work. Small things like ads block and switching off your phone can help you build these habits. Other people around you should have an idea that you have entered a distraction-free mode and you can get them informed with simple acts like closing your office door or putting on a headphone. Put away anything that can serve as a source of distraction, and your mind will begin to learn that it can do without those distractions.
3. **Keep your mind in check:** Your thoughts are some of the most subtle sources of distractions. Watch how your mind begins to wander when you are carrying out the most serious activities, even during an exam. We spend a good percentage of our mind thinking about something else while carrying out

a task. The key here is to notice when the mind is about to begin the journey and hold it back. This will mean paying a lot of attention to your mind. If there is a problem at hand that your mind keeps going back to, then you should find a solution to that problem and free your mind.

4. **Don't multitask:** Myths are flying around about the benefits of multitasking. Although some people are very proficient in the act, I do not endorse it. Multitasking is not only a distraction but a clear source of fatigue to the brain. You might feel like you have achieved more when you multitask, but when you go back, you will discover a lot of mistakes with than things that you may have thought you did right. Stopping one task and starting up another is a brain drain and focus can easily be lost.

5. **A short break will do you good:** Whenever you notice yourself getting distracted, you can take a short break and reassess the work at hand. Try to recapture the reasons why you have to remain focused on your job and give your mind a reason to concentrate. Your brain needs to be reminded about why the task at hand is important and why distractions should not even be an option.

6. **Break down the tasks into smaller fragments:** Distractions are more prone to present themselves when a project seems overwhelming. It is better for tasks to be broken down into smaller projects so that the brain is deceived into thinking the job is easier and will take a much smaller timeframe. With each accomplished project, you fell a sense of accomplishment that drives you to do more.

7. **Set Deadlines for each task:** Don't just start up a task without a deadline. Timing is everything. Give your mind and brain a timeframe to complete the task. This will give a sense of urgency, and your mind will be eager to get the job quicker.

8. **Set yourself apart:** This one goes for people who are prone to get distracted when people are around them. It is necessary to have people around you at all times, but you should also be able to identify when they constitute a distraction in your life. Before you start up a task, you can tell the people around you about how important at hand is and how much space you would love to be given. Or you can take yourself away from them

until you get the job done. They might not understand how important it may before you to complete that task successfully.
9. **Track the daily pattern of your life:** It would make sense for you to track each day's activities at night to find out how much time was spent doing what. This evaluation will quickly help you identify the distraction patterns in your life that you need to combat. When these habits have been identified, you can now start working towards creating habits that will eliminate their effect.
10. **Start early:** Earlier in this book, we talked about staying in bed until your body is ready to get up. But sometimes you need to push your body out of bed to get things done. This period of the day is best used to get your day started. There are hardly any distractions at this point, and your mind is most active and ready to perform.

7 Foods That Can Help Boost Your Brainpower

You should do everything to protect your brain and help boost its operating power. The importance of your brain cannot be overemphasized. It is in charge of a whole lot of things that go on around your body. When all of these are considered, you now discover why it is quite important to keep your brain in peak working function.

Some foods can be taken to get the brain working at its best. These foods have a lot of impact on the structure and the health of the brain. They also have some minor and major nutrients that are needed by the brain to perform to optimum levels. It has been proven over time that our body parts begin to deteriorate as we grow old, and this includes the brain, too. But even with this, you can help your brain to maintain its health as you learn to eat smarter. Some of these foods can help your brain perform better:

1. **Blueberries**

Research has shown that the flavonoids produced by this fruit are very for memory improvement. They are also known to protect the brain and reduce the effects of Alzheimer's disease and dementia. The brain also needs the antioxidants produced by the blueberries and to help improve communication among the brain cells. You can add them to your early morning cereal or squeeze out their juice.

2. Fatty Fish

The omega-3 fatty acids contained in fatty fish are known to reduce the quantity of beta-amyloid in the bloodstream. This beta-amyloid is a form of protein that forms lumps in blood vessels and the brain, thereby causing Alzheimer's disease. Omega-3 fatty acid also helps to increase the blood flow towards the brain. Some of these fishes include sardines, tuna, sardines, and salmon.

3. Broccoli

Glucosinolates contained in broccoli is broken down by the body to form isothiocyanates. These isothiocyanates are known to reduce the possibility of degenerative diseases occurring in the body. Broccoli is also very rich in flavonoids and vitamin C, which are also necessary for the brain health.

4. Turmeric

Curcumin contained in turmeric enters the brain to directly benefit the cells reproducing there. Curcumin is a potent antioxidant and anti-inflammatory compound that benefits memory system in the brain. Studies have also shown that it helps to improve the mood when it is taken.

5. Whole Grains

Whole grains are known to contain a lot of vitamins which is very important for the development of the brain and the neurological system. Whole grains include foods like barley, rice, oatmeal, and whole-grain pasta. Some of them can be taken as early cereal, or they can be boiled and taken with sauce. It is all left to your culinary imaginations.

6. Kale

Kale is another vegetable that contains glucosinolates, and just like broccoli they are also known to help reduce the body's susceptibility to degenerative diseases and keep the brain healthy and ready to function.

7. Green Tea

Caffeine, which is very important for brain function, can be found in Green tea. Taking green tea in the morning can help to give the brain a dose of alertness, memory, and focus. Another essential nutrient in green tea is L-theanine. L-theanine is an amino acid that promotes the activities of the neurotransmitter GABA. L-theanine can also help the brain relax when there has been an insanely stressful activity.

Chapter Six: Defeating Bad Habits

By now, you must have been practicing the tips given in chapters four and five about self-discipline and staying focus. Nevertheless, a conscious effort must be taken to sustain what has been learned. Thorough and sustained learning requires the learner to understand the position at which he is learning. Knowing your pace and the attitude involved is a good starting point. As it is not enough to acquire new set skills but also to identify those negative behavior pattern that ruins your productivity. These are setbacks that have been a part of your life. But what happens when you discover that the negative attitudes that frustrate your learning process are your habits? And these habits, as at when realized, have reduced the pace at which your productivity level is achieved. Our attention is not on when the bad habits started, as some began theirs at a tender age while others developed theirs as they grew into adulthood. It is a good thing that it is discovered and your statistics must have summarized the effect per time, ranging from emotional, psychological, health, etc.

Bad habits have a way of dealing with us. Some start with our inner self. It proceeds to destroy our self-image and self-worth while many others reflect on our productivity level. Whatever the effect might be, you can defeat it. You would want to know that the adverse impact of these bad habits can be so dangerous that they affect your health and mental state. And an unhealthy being can't perform to the best of his abilities.

12 BAD HABITS THAT ARE KILLING YOUR PRODUCTIVITY

1. **Trying to do every task**

Humans are not robots. And no one anticipates you to do everything. Even robots are programmed for a specific job. But more frequently than not, you tend to overwork yourself by trying out every task.

Trying something new is not bad, but doing every task is the problem. You tend to lose focus when you do that. You won't be able to boast of specialization. It would be wrong if a sales manager is seen performing the task of a personnel admin. Just as you can't eat everyone's food, so can't you do every job.

2. Letting social networks distract you

Everyone is excited at the new interface that comes with the latest update, the added filters that beautifies the sight and the one-time swipe function. And since work has taken the space of your intimate friends, getting another acquaintance who wouldn't leave anytime soon is inevitable. You then spend more of your time with them to the extent that it becomes a habit. That feeling of excitement that comes from sticking to your digital friends on the different social media platforms and the trends and updates has always been a major killer to your productive moment.

3. Clutter

You might not think of confusion as a big deal until you figure out that you can't get what you want without looking for it. Why? Because it is not organized as it ought to. An office cabinet filled with outdated reports, newspapers, and journals can add up to your work. It presents to your partner how disorganized you are. All office documents have their filing system. Littering it up with other irrelevant kinds of stuff makes everywhere untidy, and you will always need to hand yourself a search warrant.

4. Lack of a plan

Waking up into the day with the right mental attitude is good. But having no intention to fulfill the day is not a good thing to bank on. Sticking to the general plan or a plan of "no plan" is a bad habit you need to eliminate. You can't go with the flow when there is a goal to achieve. What if the general plan is not fit for your specific task?

5. Thinking of work every time

The main passion that fuels your job is the love that you have for it. But this love cannot be productive if it is not well-expressed. Thinking of work every time leaves you worried. You tend to ask yourself multiple questions at a time. What do I do next? What about the report? How do I present this paperwork? And so on. It then distracts you from creating time to plan for the work. What you have been doing is mainly anxiety.

6. First thing last, the last thing first

This sequence is a total reversal of priority. Everyone wants something, but not everyone has been able to pin their specific needs down according to how bad they need them. Generalizing what you need may not help you to do things differently. Imagine giving too many options when you can structure your needs down to the order of its importance.

7. Easy task first, hard ones later

The hard task is technically challenging, and that's why it's called that name. People tend to push the more difficult task to the future whereas, those are the most important. Getting to do the more straightforward job first, without creating a strategic plan on how to solve the harder one, pushes the task to a tight corner. It becomes harder every time it gets pushed back. Pushing an essential task to the future wouldn't make you achieve your aim. It even adds more pressure to the job.

8. Complaints

Our mental and psychological state in the workplace could be affected most times, and it is just natural for humans to get tired. And one attitude that reflects tiredness is the vocal utterance that accompanies it. Mumbling and soliloquy is a common symptom. Complaints come from a negative feeling when the right results are not achieved. And the effects of these feelings result in an unwillingness to finish the task.

9. The perfect little bit

Dedication is an attribute that shows that you value your work. This catalyst might sometimes involve adding spices to the bit that makes up perfection. Perfection is what defines our excellence. But it would be burdensome when we tend to spice up all the bits. And the bits in itself is unimportant to the result intended. What happens is that we get stuck? We get frustrated, right? Then, stress pops in.

10.   Negativity

Negativity is more of a mind thing than a physical thing, the result of which is visibly assessed. It all starts with the wrong mentality to progressively have a poor outcome. Most times, it doesn't come because someone inspired it. It comes as a reminder in your mind. It allows you to blame yourself, put yourself down. You then conclude that you are not fit to meet the target or to do any extraordinary thing. What happens is that the result will be reduced.

11.   Between the fence

A lot of times, we are faced with a great decision to make. These are choices that determine the progress of our success or an entirely purposed success. It might even be a concern that stems from the outside world but affects our immediate. A good example is when you are faced with a decision to execute a project with a handful of clients. Those which have different variables such as technicality, speed, experience, expertise, and so on. But no one wants to make the mistake of choosing the wrong one. However, not making one at all wouldn't complete the task. Your indecisiveness even prolongs the completion date.

12.   Little time to rest

A power nap is believed to revive energy and set you up to start an excellent task. So, what happens if all you got left after a hectic day is just a little time to rest? Most times, the office job is taken home as overtime. But we tend not to get the best out of the task because our body system has not been revitalized. This routine is a nasty habit that needs a second thought.

6 Ways To Eliminate Bad Habits Now

Eliminating bad habits is a great decision to take. Some have, over time, chosen to ignore their bad habits because they consider it a proper way of life. Others have found measures to manage it. Either way, life can be lived to the fullest when you are confident that no negative attitude is eating you up. Understand that it is quite possible to eliminate bad habits, and you need to be ready to do this. The following can be employed as a guide to help you out.

1. **Getting ready**

A great way to start a task is when you are fully aware of the task at hand. The same thing is with eliminating bad habits. Prepare yourself for this task. Preparing yourself means saying, "I am ready for this, and there is no better time than now." Come to the full understanding that you have signed up to do the better thing. Let it start from within you. Just like when you are inclined to think otherwise, align yourself with this new mentality that "This is my perfect time to eliminate those bad habits, and I am getting better." You might be tempted to weigh your options. Don't give it a shot. Put everything in place to get you going.

- **Think differently**

Human beings are naturally comfortable when things are easy. And for you, the bad habits must have given a bit of comfort. It's high time to think differently about the whole situation. Have a mindset that you are fighting a battle with your bad habits. Think of yourself as the soldier that is equipped with the modern-day armory and your bad habits have only stone-age weapons. With this mindset alone, you have already placed yourself in a position of victory. All other steps that will be taken will not be considered grievous.

- **Intentionality**

A deliberate attitude needs to be asserted here. You need to stand for this new movement regardless of any challenge that may accompany this exercise. Activate the power of the mind to achieve the great result of breaking those bad habits

2. The Snail Approach

If there is anything the snail is known for, it is its slowness in movement. No one is suggesting to you to get a snail (you might if you want to). But the snail approach brings an understanding that you have to start small. And starting small sometimes might appear slow. Understand that your new habit will not come as a "big bang" but in a steady-state. Your aim at this level is progress. Ensure that you are doing something different from the old habit. There is no need to rush.

3. Identify the why

You might not have thought about why you do the things you do, maybe just because it has become a part of you. Get settled and identify those things that trigger you to do what you do. Maybe you overthink your job anytime you receive a new mail. Or you actively stay on social networks whenever you have a dispute with your friend. Just identify the triggers behind those bad habits, and you have started the elimination process already.

- **Evaluate**

A sincere appraisal of your negative behavior is necessary at this stage. Sincerely weigh the consequences of these behaviors with the right one. You would agree that the positive sides far outweigh the negative. Don't crucify yourself when you have a setback. It is an expectation that is likely to happen. Ensure you get back on track

4. Create reminders

One of the first drives that support our commitment is when we are constantly reminded of it. You need to be reminded that you want to eliminate these bad habits. It will not only help you at present, but will also create an atmosphere for a great future.

- **Digital reminders**

Pushing a reminder can work well with most mobile devices. You can search for apps that create a to-do list, look up the options and enable the alarm function. Create a word or phrase that continually reminds you of the habit to break. It's quite evident that, by now, you must have identified the cause or triggers of your bad habit. If yours is staying on the social networks often, you may want to have a word that says, "it's time to sleep." Or if you are fond of negativity, you might have this: "My negative thought pattern will not help me, I deserve happiness, and that's what will work for me." Ensure you set the alarm at least 10 minutes before the beginning of your extremes. You will know when you are about getting there. This well-structured strategy will create enough time for you to adjust effectively.

- **Journaling**

Writing things out yourself will give you a sense of personalizing your target. Get a journaling book in the book store or create one for yourself. Divide the page into two vertically. Start with writing your noted terrible habits on the first side. Add reminders of what you should do (or not do) on the other side. This idea models the digital reminder. You could analyze your progress by ticking the habit you are constantly reminded of.

- **Friends**

You might consider telling your friend about this move. There is always a friend that pushes us until a task is done successfully. He/she might even come up with better suggestions or plan. This action will give you a sense of accountability. Ensure you inform your friend to provide you with a progress report, or you could come up with a guide yourself. He wouldn't want you to be ridiculed with failure. Not again!

- **Stickers**

Inscribe short words/phrases on labels and fix it around you. The little sticky note scattered around you will serve a perfect reminder of what you need to do. Ensure you attach it where your bad habit triggers. It can be in your office, on your calendar, notepad, on the wall and even in your car.

5.   **Switch your surroundings**

Visiting a particular place might be the trigger to one of your bad habits. You tend to drink more bottles of beer whenever you hang out with friends at the local bar downtown. Consider going to another bar, different from the one you frequent, this time alone. Create a new atmosphere for yourself. Sometimes, the feel of a place you continuously visit pushes you to react negatively.

- **Rewarding every broken habit**

"Broken habit" here means that you have been able to stop the practice successfully. You are no longer seen doing it. Motivate your progress into positivity by rewarding yourself. Everyone needs encouragement. And this reward system may be the only thing that will keep you going till you achieve maximum success.

- **Substitute**

A meaningful way to reward yourself is to look for a positive habit that will substitute the bad habit. A habit is a part of your life. Just like the game of football, the less effective player is replaced; but in urgent cases, a dire need to change the fit player is inevitable when the strategy does not seem to work. It is the same here. Change the less productive habit to have a more productive life.

You would also agree that those bad habits come with fulfillment. Most times, it is there to fulfill a need that might come as a result of depression, sadness, rejection, failure, boredom, etc. if those needs are not met with another thing, then, there is a loophole.

- **Draft a plan and strategize**

Know what to do the when triggers immediately come up. Work with the strategy of reward system any time you replace your bad habit with the positive pattern. Don't give space for loneliness. Loneliness in this regard means dissatisfaction in your expectations. Don't expect to be in that mess again. This practice would be quite more comfortable for you when you avoid the triggers

- **Look out to the future**

The future you are looking out for is someone else's reality, and some people are doing what you want to achieve now. Why not move close to them and make new friends. If restraining yourself from your old friends will give you enough time to break off from your bad habits, you need to give it a shot.

6. **Seek professional support**

If you still find it challenging to adopt a positive attitude towards the effort of helping yourself, consider seeing a professional. The psychologist can help identify psychological, emotional, and behavioral patterns that trigger bad habits. He will ensure your progress and can be accounted to.

6 Ways To Create Great Habits That Stick

You may have wondered why your plans are not working as expected. It may have worked for some time, but it looks dull and does not seem to work. You may have told yourself to stop staying 8 hours a day on the internet without learning something new, but it seems not to work. Do not fret. Come to a new awareness that this is a different game for you. It's not the game of chance but total commitment. Be sure that you have been able to discover what triggers your bad habits and the estranging patterns behind it. You might need to analyze your pursuit and the sacrifice behind it. "What do I want and how bad do I want it to change my life?" Have a breakdown of what you will be doing more and what will be done less. Tell your inner self the truth that needs to be told. This is you looking forward to the future of positivity. This is a sure way to get started.

Stop Procrastination

1. Focus on one habit at a time

Since your habits didn't start all at once, you need to know that changing it won't be all at once either, as much as you want it to be. Try tackling one habit at a time. If your focus is to stop the negative attitude towards project execution, face it. Don't combine many things. It's even an unhealthy attitude to try doing many things together

Start with the habit you are most uncomfortable with. Don't be in a rush. Progress is what you are after. Once you know the course you are following, getting there won't be a problem.

2. Ask questions

Don't act as if you are a professional here. There are so many things that will be going through your mind. Ask! You might be wondering how you would survive the night without excessive alcohol. Ask: "What if I would survive the first four hours?" Asking questions should not be limited to you. The help of a therapist or psychologist could be of help. You could also find it helpful when you ask questions from someone who has stuck to the new habit you are about to learn.

Your curiosity might also want to know when you will be able to adapt to the new habit. Ask! This way, you can make up your mind since you know the "when," "how," and "why."

3. Start with a deadline

We have established that there is no need to rush through sticking to positive habits. But you can start small and at your own pace. Give yourself a deadline to try out the first habit. Let's say for twenty days. So, for the next twenty days, you won't make that specific habit you have decided to start with. And of course, you'd replace it with the positive one. You can monitor your progress with your fingers. Your fingernails can represent the first ten days. Get a designed nail sticker and fix it to your fingernails daily after successfully sticking to the positive habit. After the sticker must have been attached for the first ten days, start removing them daily till the end of the next ten days. This action plan will give you a sense of control. You will have been able to both personalize this exercise and at the same time give it a deadline.

4. Celebrate your progress

You have started on a "big cheque" "less work" model. The big cheque represents your aspired habit, while less work is your effort to make things better. Realize that your goal is big but achievable. Achieving your aim progressively shows that you have moved from the realm of fantasy to reality. So why not celebrate every purpose you achieve? Boost your motivation by celebrating every progress. This tells you that you can do more and even better.

5. Stay with the tune

The rhythm of the new habit has been on the air for some time. Make sure you continue to dance to the song. No other song should persuade you. You have to be consistent. You might not want to change your routine. Try to build your purposed habit according to your method. All you require to do is to put on the new initiative. You might be thinking of decluttering your wardrobe. You could effectively do this the very moment you want to dress up. Just pick your preferred dress and use the other hand to arrange the other suits. Remember, start small so that you won't be overwhelmed.

6. Don't give too many options

Being specific on strategies to stick to your new habit is necessary. Once you decide on how you want to go about it, stick to the plan. The moment you start weighing many options, doubt may set in. You might even get confused and discouraged. You have decided to reduce your alcohol intake by taking one full lemon after a glass of beer. Good! Stick to it. There are many other important decisions to make than to begin to conflict the ones you have already made.

Chapter Seven: Taming The Mind

The human mind is naturally wild and always in need of an adventure. Because of this, it is necessary that you learn how to tame the mind and have it work to your advantage. This will help it work to your advantage and provide you with lots of positivity. One of the wisest teachers and psychologists of all time, Buddha, described the human mind as a monkey that is always jumping about screeching and chattering endlessly. We all have minds that never want to rest, always in need of something else. Just as a monkey is always in need of attention, the human mind to always want you to put your entire focus on it. It achieves its goals in different ways, such as overhanging, negative considerations, anxiety, and fear.

Due to the presence of this monkey mind, it has now become harder for us to live in the present. Most of our time as humans is spent either regretting about the past or living in fear of the future. Soon you discover that you have become unhappy, sad, naturally angry, and restless. It is time to calm down and tame the monkey in mind. After all, it is your mind, and you should make use of it like you actually possess it. Some simple benefits of taming your mind include:

- Clarity of mind
- Full happiness
- Better sleep
- Focus and concentration
- etc.

All of these are very excellent benefits, and you should not hesitate to embrace them into your life. But there are some minor steps I will show you to help you fully actualize this dream.

12 Essential Tips To Stop Overthinking And Control Your Mind

It might sound strange to you, but the truth is that you are probably addicted to thinking. You may have never started to consider it, but most of us do spend a lot of time thinking and overworking our minds. We think about what to eat for dinner, which seasons to continue on Netflix, why the world climate is changing so severely. We think about virtually everything. While thinking is an excellent and necessary venture, it can sometimes clog up the mind when it becomes too much. Most of the time, we never know that it has become too much, and that is where the problem lies. Thinking so much in your mind can become a slight disorder and turn you towards overwhelming anxiety. Your mind stays stressed, and peace begins to elude you. Practice these and come up with your testimony:

1. **Study your mind and find those things that cause you stress and anxiety**

There are different reasons for different people as to why they overthink. For some, it could be financial instability; for others, security reasons; and for still others, it could be a terminal sickness. You will need to find yours. Ask yourself the necessary questions why you overthink, and the times you are most likely to overthink. Take note of the major things you think of and the pattern in which all of those thoughts form themselves. If this is done diligently, your notes will help you figure out some of the major reasons why you are currently overthinking.

2. **Consider the things that make you overthink**

The question here is, how important are those things that make you overthink? What use will they play in your life is you continue to trouble your mind about them? Will it matter in four years or four months even? If the answer is no, you should snap out of it. Your mind is simply playing sad tricks with you, and you have to be the boss here.

If they are not important, then you should stop thinking about them and focus your time on more important things.

3. **Make quick decisions**

Learn to make a quick decision and get the process over with. If you are a kind of person that can take hours trying to figure out what to eat for lunch, then this is for you. There should be a timeframe for decision-making in your life. If you are going for a vacation, do your research and settle the destination in one week. Don't allow it linger on and on and become a problem to you.

4. **Start the day on a proper note**

I have mentioned it before: bad mornings will most likely lead to a bad day. Take hold of your day from the morning and begin to eliminate any stressful thoughts that make want to raise their heads. You can do this by reading something that will uplift your spirit every morning, or you can practice meditation to calm your mind.

5. **Understand that overthinking is bad for your mental health**

Overthinking steals away all of your time and energy that should have been used for something more important. It leaves you drained and unable to achieve tangible results. By doing some of these things to your mental health, you become susceptible to anxiety and depression, which are some major triggers of suicides and suicidal thoughts.

6. **Don't get too excited**

Of course, people also overthink positive thoughts. For instance, you have just carried out a short survey of your business profit projection and have seen that you could get thousands of dollars richer before the year ends. You begin to imagine all the things you could do with the money, the good life you can finally have, and the things you can finally get rid of. These thoughts will consume you with baseless excitement to the extent that you might forget ideas and continue to ruminate on them over and over, basking in the beauty you imagine for yourself.

7. **Document your thoughts**

Get those thoughts out of your head and into a paper. It helps out sometimes. You can get a notepad close to your bed and jot down those thoughts that come to you whenever you are about to go into sleep. Once it has been put down, the brain will be forced to let go of it and free you.

8. **Adopt a more carefree lifestyle**

Sometimes it is best not to care. Sure, there are a lot of things that should bother you, but ask yourself how many times thinking over a situation has helped that situation. The chances are one in a million. So sometimes it is best you forget everything and live like a king. Distract yourself from your thoughts and try to practice happiness more often.

9. **Get busy**

The mind rarely ever has time to think when you are busy. Although it can still happen, that will only come as a form of distraction which I have taught you how to overcome. One major cause of overthinking is an unproductive mind. People who keep themselves busy hardly ever have enough time to allow them to mind wander towards baseless thoughts.

10. **Realize that you can't control everything**

There are things that you can control, and there are others that are simply out of your control league. You have a journey tomorrow, and the weather forecasts that it will be a rainy day. There is no need to stress yourself over it. Cancel the trip if need be and have peace of mind.

11. **Purge Your Environment of overthinkers**

Your environment may play a significant role in triggering overthinking. It doesn't just stop at the people close to you. It extends to the things you read, the podcasts you listen to, the trends you follow, etc. Remove all of these from your immediate environment.

12. **Live in the present (not in the past or future)**
The only things that should bother you are those things that are presently going on in your life. If you are in college, focus on your studies and get good grades. Prepare for the future and stop bothering about it. If you were molested as a child, find a way to forgive and move on with your life. It can be hard, but remember, it is all for you.

7 Techniques To Conquer The Fear Of Failure

It is natural to fear failure. Failure is never something that one would want to be associated with, and so humans shake in their boots at the sight of it. Once we are pushed outside of our comfort zone, we begin to feel that things can probably go wrong. And the truth is that failure's sting is painful and it can leave you with a blemish for the rest of your life, except if you are a person that heals quickly and moves on fast. Understand that your failures are always a springboard to your success. You might be running out of time, but that is enough reason why you should do away with the fear of failure and instead calm down. Without darkness, you will never understand light. Without cold, you will never appreciate the heat. Without failure, you will never understand the true essence of success. So, there is no need to fear failure per se. But conquering the fear of failure isn't as easy as that. You need to understand and put some things in place to fully gain the upper hand. Some of these include:

1. **Understand that failing doesn't mean that you are a failure**
A lot of people have failed a lot of times, but today we don't see them as failures. The examples are numerous.

- Nobody knows how many times Edison tried until he was finally able to invent the incandescent light bulb. But it is believed that it was more than a hundred times.

Stop Procrastination

- An editor once told Walt Disney that his animations lacked imagination. Today, the Walt Disney company has more than fifty hugely successful animated films under its belt.
- J.K. Rowling's Harry Potter series was rejected more than ten times by different publishers until luck found her. Today she is the wealthiest author alive.

There are more examples, but the bottom line is that failure is never an endpoint except if you have decided for it to become your endpoint.

2. **Learn from your failures**

No matter how negative and experience is, there is always something positive to learn from it. It is only a fool that makes the same mistake twice. Sieve out all of our failures and select the benefits. They are there. You only have to look deeper and catch them. One way that can help you out is to begin to write out all the ventures that you failed in and write out the things you may have learned from failing in them.

3. **View any sight of failure as a challenge to step up your game**

If you think you might fail, take up the challenge, and prepare yourself not to fail. That is the only way to success. In fact, only a handful of people are totally sure of success when they first started out a venture. Most of the time, they were quite pessimistic, but they put in their best and hoped for success. Success hardly eludes people like that, except if there was a mistake made somewhere.

4. **Stay optimistic and keep visualizing success**

Push the thought of failure away from your mind by stay positive and thinking positivity. The thought of failing will surely come, but what if you succeed? There are two sides to this coin, and none of them should be neglected while viewing the coin. If one out of every hundred business startups in our community survives more than five years, then it could be your startup. If only one person succeeds, then it could be you.

Stop Procrastination

5. Understand that the fear of failure doesn't make you a success

No matter how much you sit about achieve nothing because of failure, success will never pity you and come to your rescue. Oh, you think the fear of failure is a heavy burden to bear? Try the burden of regret and see how far that will carry you. There is nothing as painful as seeing somebody achieving the things you had always wanted to achieve, just because you allowed the fear of failure to hold you back. Shove failure off you back and make a move.

6. Be kind to yourself

If you have ever experienced failure people before, it is time to get over it. Learn from your failures and get over it. Your mind might want to keep reminding you about how bad you are, telling you that you will never be good at anything. Instead, be kind to yourself. If you made a mistake in the past, promise yourself not to go down the same part again. Then forge ahead. Nobody is ever above mistakes.

7. Avoid perfectionism

Nothing in the world is ever perfect. Every beautiful thing in the world is laced with some flaw or the other. Recognize that nothing you will ever do will be downright perfect, so go ahead and start up something. Complete the task with the mistakes and then take the time to correct the mistakes. Completing the project itself is one great step, and this will give you the urge to carry on.

6 Secrets For Creating A Success Mindset

There can never be success without a success mindset. Those two go together like smoke and fire. There can never be one without the other. Think about most of the successful people that you know. The chance that they enter into success by mistake is pretty slim. A lot of the time, people who have a failure mindset always end up in failure, because they hardly ever identify opportunities whenever they meet them. A failure mindset will always work against you. No matter how much

Stop Procrastination

you try, no matter all the hard work you put in place, a mind running on failure will always produce failure. One major factor that differentiates great achievers from failures is the way they think, the content of their minds. So, to create the success you need, you need to prepare your mind for it. A failure mindset will always be shocked when success is finally achieved, but a success mindset will see success coming from a mile off. These secrets will help you develop the perfect mindset that will accommodate success:

1. Achieve small goals one at a time

When you look at your one big dream, the size of it might scare you into thinking you might fail in the long run. Remember that the large success picture does not appear at the snap of a finger. Rome was not built in a day. It was built one stone at a time. What are the stones that will build your future? Start putting them in, one block at a time. You want to win the Nobel Prize in Physics, then, you have to have a college degree in Physics first. You want to become a Pulitzer Award winner for Fiction; then, you must begin writing that novel now. These small blocks will build into one great mountain of success.

2. Take charge of your mind

We have touched little about this in Chapter 7 (taming the mind). It is easier for the mind to envision failure than to envision success. Close your eyes and imagine a plain ground, a desert without any form of life. See how easy that is to do? Now close your eyes and imagine that desert with skyscrapers, with people of all races engaging themselves in commerce. Imagine that this desert contains the tallest building in the world. See how hard it is for your mind to create a picture of wealth and abundance. If you succeeded, it must have taken you a conscious effort to do so. This is the kind of effort required to see your life as a success.

3. Be flexible and ready to tweak your plans

There is no hundred percent success plan in the world. Things can go wrong and show you the flaws in your plans. At this point, the best thing to do is to keep your mind ready for a change. It is possible that you will not achieve all the goals you attached to a plan, and that is ok. All you have to do is make sure that your mind is always ready for a change of plan.

4. You are your biggest competition

Always strive to get ahead of yourself. Know your destination and find out how fast you should move, then, move in that pace. Measuring yourself to the achievements of others can leave you with detrimental consequences. You can look up to people who have gone ahead of you and admire their lifestyle. Learn from them and keep trying to develop yourself.

5. Find a Mentor (someone that will keep you motivated)

A mentor is someone who acts like a parent to you or a master in any given field or endeavors you may find yourself. Put yourself in positions where you get to meet the best of the best in your field. Then build strong relationships with them that will turn into a mentorship. A mentor will be someone you can easily report yourself to if you make a mistake. A mentor will both scold and advise you whenever needed. And knowing that you have someone you can always look up to will provide with the needed dose of success mindset to keep you going.

6. Talk to yourself

The best advice you can get is the one you give to yourself. Sit yourself down and talk to you. Ask all the necessary questions and try to find out why things are working out the way that they are supposed to. The key here is that you have to be truthful with yourself. Take time and encourage yourself. Reward yourself. Appreciate yourself. Tell yourself you have to work harder and achieve better results. These will continually drive to achieve more at any given time.

Chapter 8: Planing For Your Success

The general public does not have the same definition of success, but in a broad view, doing well in the course of action can be tagged as a success. Some are of the school of thought that success has the right outcome from a decision; a superb result after an intention is fulfilled. However you define as successful living, be sure that some elements must be seen in it. Some of them are dedication, goal setting, motivation, and problem-solving. None of these traits will be found on a path to fulfillment if you don't understand the intent behind success.

Understanding your intent gives a sense of direction. You now have a decision tool to work with. You could predict where you are coming to your destination. You may ask, "What pushes me to set those unattainable targets? Why do I envision to become muscular? "Maybe I just stumbled on it," you may reply. Ask yourself many of these questions. Comprehend what moves you. From here, the energy to keep moving towards the rough road of attainment is fueled continuously. You may not need another person to push you to fulfillment. You and the inner drive will be enough motivation to get going.

Well, success is intentional, and you could get prepared for it. That's what this chapter promises to unleash.

6 Techniques To Succeed At Goal Setting

1. **See the birds before the sky**

Don't get me wrong here. We live in a world of no limitations, and everything is possible. But you need to see the things that are closer to you first before you can reach out to things beyond. Go for a goal you can easily attain. No rule says you must start in a hard way. And you don't have to be so complicated when planning for your goals. Achieve the little ones you can now, and the motivation will keep you inspired for the bigger ones.

2. **Expand your horizon**

Get your imagination to work. See yourself beyond the present level you are now. Until your inner self is motivated to achieve greatness, it will be difficult, if not impossible, to go far. Access as much information as possible to hit your goals. A better way to map out your plan is when vitality is added to the specific target.

3. **Admit your setbacks**

Aiming for perfection comes with loads of experience. You would not be experienced all at once in a day. What you call constant failure is what sets you on the peak. For you to move forward in fulfilling your goals, accept at every point when you fail. Acknowledging failures allows you to review your actions as well as find solutions for them. Unless you take your wrongs, you can't see the right.

4. **See it the other way round**

There is no cause to beat around the bush when the solution seems far. Don't get too complacent about your goal attainment. If you are stuck at an end, think of other ways to go about it. Be flexible! Sometimes, your deadline might have exceeded beyond a reasonable doubt. Get yourself going. Remember that what you want to achieve is still possible. If your goal is to study five chapters of a book in five days, and at the end of the sixth day, you are still in chapter four. Do not be discouraged and don't feel wrong about not meeting your target. Pick up the section for the next day. Ensure you review the cause of the delay and move on.

5. **Be result-oriented**

What should drive you is the success behind the goal. You will likely face distractions. It may come from your workplace, environment, or friends. Whatever it is, it shouldn't you stop from what you have set your mind to achieve. Think and position your brain for positivity. See every challenge as an avenue to become better. Visualize your results even before attaining them. Create a sound memory for yourself. Take pictures of what you tag as a success. Hang it around you, and let it encourage you now and then. It will not only boost your alertness; it will also make the journey to attainment fun

6. Don't get distracted

When it comes to priority, goals are not seeds of different fruits in a basket. They should be seen as fruits of a seed. Give preferences to what you want to achieve, and allow it to give birth to other goals. This approach ensures that you are orderly in your way to secure productivity. One big distraction you won't see coming is when you are trying to do many things at a time.

5 Less-Known Goal-Setting Tips Straight From The Experts

To fetch a glass of water seems more relaxed than setting a goal sometimes. But it may seem so difficult after writing your targets, and not attaining them. It might be a long-term goal or short-term. Yours might range from career to life goals. All the same, frustration may set in when none of these look attainable. The following tips will guide you to succeed in goal setting.

1. Understand yourself

Socrates emphasized the subject of "self-knowledge." He believed that no one could be helped without self-identification. Although, major upgrades in science and technology has given a lot of answers to these worrying questions. Nonetheless, the wisdom behind getting to know the kind of human being you are is essential. It is a factor to consider for one to be successful in the course of attaining targets. Do a quick analysis of your components.

- Start by asking questions

What are you made of? Why do I think differently from others? What causes me to get anxious over little subjects? Why do I get nervous anytime I see strangers? Questions like this could not be asked until you have taken time to think of some things you often do. The aim here is not for you to feel inadequate or depressed. It is just for you to get better.

- Analyze your findings

Check your social, spiritual, health, physical, psychological, and intellectual capabilities. A game of comparison will not work here. This check is for you! What am I capable of doing? And at what pace am I capable of doing it? What makes me learn fast with little energy? "I think I sleep faster whenever I take cereals." "Oh! I doze off almost immediately whenever I rub lotion on my feet." Analyzing will give you enough reasons why you do what you do.

- Make more findings

Don't stop at your discovery. Do more research online. Find out if the traits you saw in yourself is found in other people too. How were they able to overcome it? Was it by themselves, or were they helped by a friend or professional? Is this a childhood behavior or it accompanies growing up to adulthood? Getting answers to those questions, and many more you would like to add gives you a sense of identification.

- Combine factors

You could make a temporary conclusion base on your findings. By now, you are sure that what you feel and how you feel is reasonable. Maybe what you discovered has shown to you that you need help. Good! You are making progress. Don't combine any information if you have not researched extensively. Put each of these inputs together and help yourself with it.

2. Have a clear definition of your goal

Stop Procrastination

What we sometimes see as a path can sometimes be blockage. We may tend to see possibilities at achieving a goal, but in the end, the result appears disappointing. Here is the reason. Humans have failed to properly decide without any form of prejudice what they want out of life. It is not as easy as we think, but this is what makes the goal attainment frustrating.

- Identify the difference

Just because it is achievable does not mean it has the same strategy as other goals. Understand the difference between what is to be achieved in a short while and what is to be met for a lifetime. Define what your goal is in your terms. What someone considers as a short-term goal may be a long-term goal for you. A long-term goal cannot be achieved if it is not broken down into smaller bits. There is no technicality in this at all. A short-term goal is what you want to reach over a short period while a long-term goal will take a more extended period to attain (it can be for months or years). Your friend, who dreams of becoming a chartered accountant, may plan to go to business school for that purpose. If you are not aware that going to business school is a strategy to pursue a career goal (which is to become a chartered accountant), you might follow suit and get frustrated at the end.

- Strategize and break down the difference

For every future, there is always a day to start it. That day is the present day you are in right now. And in a full day comprises of hours, minutes and seconds. Do a justification of what is to be done presently (at this very second) that will help the next 1,220 hours that you have set the deadline.

What you should have accomplished in the next few days should not be muddled up with next years'. You don't have to get worried over the next decade when you can successfully fulfill the project for the next day.

Your action plan might be to extract a picture of a baby and gum it at the back of your door together with an adult image. Seeing those pictures should remind you of this guide.

- Have a clear direction

This point is where decision-making is essential. Gain the confidence to know what you want. Don't forget that your composition is not only psychological. You have to be specific enough in each area of your life.

- Decide and define what you want

What do I want in life? What do I want out of life? Ask yourself those questions. Money or comfort? Some might say both. But the truth is that what we want is a comfort. And we feel that getting the kind of pleasure we want needs money to achieve it. That's true! The idea is this: We don't want our bodies to be stressed. We want our vacation to be around the cutest places around the world. The sea view apartment has always been our dream residence. Those kinds of comforts that riches can get might not sit well with some people.

Giving to orphanages gives some people relief. Donating to NGOs might give confidence to some. So, define what you want and don't get confused because of someone else's needs. Your discovery should not be stacked to your head alone. Help yourself by writing it down. Your journal or diary might be a great friend to gist with.

- Identify the process involved

Attaining a goal is not automatic. It doesn't come as we project many times. There are steps to take to be successful in it. Ensure that you maximize each process fully before going to the next. You might have set a target to read three chapters of book per day. Until you have mastered consistency in reading those three chapters, you shouldn't think of increasing your reading goals to five chapters.

- Fill the gap

Get motivated to keep going. Whenever it seems like you have missed your routine to attaining goals, get a substitute to make up for it. It might involve doing a review or progress check on your previous goals. You might decide to get more information about what you have been doing recently. Ensure that you are not lagging. Note that you are not supposed to take this as a perfect excuse for shirking responsibilities.

3. Take the first step and continue

Nothing can be as hard as having the courage to begin. Having made a proper analysis of who you are, and what you are capable of doing, you are well aware of your mental and intellectual capabilities now. It is time to put them to work.

Start with your skills. Everyone has something they are good with. And you are no exception. Commit your passion to your skills by discovering what will help you to do more. Our aim here is for you to channel those skills to ease your goal setting

4. Get a model

Imagine how a child thinks when he is writing with a pencil. It's easy at first, because his hand was held while writing. Attaining goals can be the same when there is a structure to follow.

- External model

Life is practical, so is everything that exists in it. Your big motivation might spark up from getting a life model. This model is someone who has excelled in your proposed project. You might decide to choose a leader from your workplace or in your social group. The attributes of a leader should be more inspirational than a boss. Discover one in the path of your pursuit. It might even be at your religious gathering. One of the beautiful things to discover in a model is the ready-made pattern to follow. It is more like having a template to work with. With it, life becomes more real to you. You will tend to find proper guidance on what you do.

- Be your greatest asset

It is good that there is someone around to check on us. But the biggest motivation we would get is the energy from within us. No one can encourage you more than yourself. Inspire yourself to greatness. See yourself as a helper and the one that needs help. It is a contemporary approach to solving the problem. You are both the counselor and the client. Think of the kind of advice you would give to a distressed friend. Give such to yourself when you are in distress. It might not come easy at first. Don't forget that this is your first attempt. A better way to make it go well is for you to write down crucial advice you have given before. You should be able to devise relevant admonitions that have lifted people's spirit at one time. Use them for yourself. Also, think of the congratulatory message you sent to your relative at a time when he/she did something spectacular. Say it to yourself too.

5. Review your progress

Always have it in mind that your development is significant. Do a routine review of your goal. Ask relevant questions such as the process, the resources, sacrifice, and time involved. Don't pretend as if you have not been doing anything. Go through the first tip in this section again, and apply it to your review strategy.

7 Important Steps To Plan For Success

Successful living is not accidental. And to break the barrier of failed principles, you need a new awareness. Define your success, understand the purpose, and we can both work on a plan. This approach will help open up the ability to affect change in your life. It has to come as a choice for personal development.

1. Get ready mentally

There are realities to successful living, and one of them has to start within us. You need to be prepared mentally. This means that you have settled your mind on achieving success. And being successful is the only option you have. Prepare your mind to execute a different task that will require sacrifice. There will be a reshuffle of time spent, friends to hang out with, and certain things to do at a particular period. Create that positive mindset to overcome any challenges when it surfaces. You might need to develop many skills that you are not familiar with. Be ready to embrace failure as a stepping stone to become better. Quitting should not be an escape route to failure.

2. Maintain an expressed goal

Being specific about the kind of success you want is a better way to plan it. Express it by writing it down. You might decide to make it more professional. Structure it as a statement. Let it be as transparent as possible. Combine the right words that will set your foot running. Don't write any statement that seems too general. Let it unveil your intention to achieve results.

3. Employ resources

It is expected that confusion will set in during the journey of success. Getting ready for such is a way to show that we are prepared for it. Seek out for influencers around you. Some people have been where you are planning to be. Discover one of them and subscribe to their teaching. Go online and sign up for emails that are relevant to your plans. Listen and follow TV shows that deal with finance and investment. Streaming several videos on YouTube wouldn't be a bad idea either.

4. Secure a plan

By now, you should have been able to gather enough knowledge to give you an edge. Design a strategy that will most fit you. Don't forget that you don't need to generalize your methods, and starting small is something you shouldn't forget so soon. Realize the opportunities that lie in fulfilling every strategy and take it.

5. Invest in time

By now, you should have been able to identify your priorities. Priority is very crucial in planning for success. You don't just focus on a thing without creating extra time to make it work. During this time, do more research about your plans, review them, and meditate over them. Learn what you need to know about specific action and develop yourself in it.

6. Boosters

See and create enough motivation to keep you going. Start with your willpower. Settle every inner craving. You don't want to have setbacks again, do you? No! Then, set boosters for yourself. Don't forget that no one can give you true happiness than yourself. The same thing is real with motivation. Have reasons to find joy in your strategies to success, and that's why it is best to adopt a plan that most fits you. You may extend a bit of your motivation to your friend. This action will work well when you report your progress to them, and at every development, they reward you (based on mutual consent).

You might go the extra mile of creating what I tagged as "progress competition." It means trying to get better results at every little success. This effort will always bring consciousness to become better because you continuously see the next achievement as an upgrade to the previous. Your focus here is to ensure the consistent improvement in every course of action

7. Learn from tactics

The world revolves around ideas, and through that, innovations are born. Study world leaders and successful individuals. There are specific attributes that make them stand out in their respective fields. You may adopt some of their principles. If it performed for them, it would surely be a perfect guide for you too.

30 Day Step-By-Step Plan To Help You Build Habits And Fire Up Your Productivity

I believe that you have had a most amazing time going through the contents of this book. Some of the things that have listed here are small bits of the things you can do to fire up your creativity. By now you should be putting things in place to be able to conquer your distractions, create more focus and stay motivated. We know that random practices do not easily lead to success. There has to be a set-down plan to get the best out of ever set of instructions. Because of this, I have decided to gift you this 30-day step-by-step plan to enhance your creativity, motivation and productivity. This plan is loaded with small points that will change your life one day at a time for the next thirty days. All you have to do is follow it strictly and don't falter at any point, no matter how weary you may get.

This aspect of the book has been broken down into 30 parts, representing the thirty days in which the steps will be taken. You might wonder if it is really necessary to take it one day at a time. Well, it is up to you. If you have already conquered one day of the plan, you can move over to the next. Even after experiencing success, please do not forsake the instructions contained here. Go over them from time to time, probably every 60 days or as you may see fit. Take this as a guide. You know yourself best and you know how these guidelines will suit. Do not hesitate to modify them however you see fit. Don't forget to stick to every habit you are developing during these thirty days. It will change your life. I wish you success.

Day 1	Day 2

Morning
  1. Exercise the body for about 10 minutes.
  2. Listen to a motivating podcast.
	Morning
	  1. Clear work desk at work.
	  2. Skip and exercise the body for twenty minutes.
	  3. Repeat some positive affirmations to myself.

3. Eat a well-balanced diet from the list of highly energetic foods (example: Brown rice and Sweet Potatoes). 4. Get the mind to work. Afternoon 1. Study the task at hand and try to identify the benefits open to me if I am able to complete the specific task. 2. Have a short power nap. 3. Read a book and refresh the mind.	Afternoon 1. Try to find ways and reasons to love my job even better. 2. Break major tasks into bits. 3. Set a timeframe to complete each bit of broken-down tasks. 4. Do away with anything that may present itself as some sort of escape route from the task at hand.
Day 3	Day 4
Morning 1. Clear work desk at work. 2. Skip and exercise the body for twenty minutes. 3. Repeat some positive affirmations to myself. Afternoon 1. Study the task at hand and try to identify the benefits open to me if I am able to complete the specific task. 2. Have a short power nap. 3. Read a book and refresh the mind. Evening	Morning 1. Listen to a motivating podcast. 2. Clear work desk at work. Afternoon 1. Let off a little steam doing something fun like listening to music, taking a walk with the dog, or conversing with a co-worker. 2. Have a short power nap if I feel tired or a little stressed out. This will help replenish my mind. 3. Try to reduce the workload at hand by pushing some to a later time.

1. Make a short assessment of my major life goals and see how far I have come towards achieving them. 2. Evaluate the day and scold myself of any mistakes made.	Note: You are not procrastinating. You are only trying to provide your mind with the necessary clarity needed to complete a particular task. Evening 1. Reread chapter six of this book and find out how well I have been coping with the instructions.
Day 5	Day 6
Morning 1. Creatively combine any of the energy boosting foods listed in chapter one. Afternoon 1. Break major tasks into bits. 2. Set a timeframe to complete each bit of broken-down tasks. 3. Do away with anything that may present itself as some sort of escape route from the task at hand. Evening 1. Evaluate the day and scold myself of any mistakes made. 2. Make important decisions for the next day this evening.	Morning 1. Listen to a motivating podcast. 2. No screen time until I complete a major task. Afternoon 4. Study the task at hand and try to identify the benefits open to me if I am able to complete the specific task. 5. Have a short power nap. 6. Read a book and refresh the mind. Evening 1. Evaluate the day and scold myself of any mistakes made. 2. Go through chapter four of this book and remind yourself of its contents.
Day 7	Day 8
Morning	Morning

1. Creatively combine any of the energy boosting foods listed in chapter one. Afternoon 1. Take a short power nap. 2. Eat brain fruits like blueberries. 3. Spend one hour completing a major task. Evening 1. Spend the evening brainstorming with people in my field who can be good mentors. 2. Figure out practical ways in which I can connect to them and make them pick interest in helping me out.	1. Meditate for 10 straight minutes. 2. Clean and declutter my home and workspaces to give myself some form of clarity. 3. Perform the most tedious task this morning. Evening 1. Create a list of activities for the next day. 2. Read one chapter from any book. 3. Watch an inspiring video.
Day 9	Day 10
Morning 1. Listen to a motivating podcast. 2. Creatively combine any of the energy boosting foods listed in chapter one. Afternoon 1. Break major tasks into bits.	Morning 1. Take a glass of water first thing this morning. 2. No screen time this morning until I have completed one particular task completely. Afternoon 1. Call my mentor and talk to them about my progress. 2. Complete one part of a major task.

2. Set a timeframe to complete each bit of broken-down tasks. 3. Do away with anything that may present itself as some sort of escape route from the task at hand. Evening 1. Go through chapter one of this book and remind myself of its contents.	Evening 1. Read chapter two of this book and assess how well I have followed the instructions. 2. Answer emails and reply messages.
Day 11	Day 12
Morning 1. Meditate for 15 straight minutes. Afternoon 1. Take a short power nap. 2. Eat brain fruits like blueberries. 3. Spend one hour completing a major task. Evening 1. List out things I am grateful for. 2. Reward myself with something pleasurable.	Morning 1. No screen time until 9am. 2. Begin a major task. Afternoon 1. Take a short power nap. 2. Eat brain fruits like blueberries. 3. Spend one hour completing a major task. Evening 1. Go through chapter seven of this book and remind yourself of its contents. 2. Go to bed early for the next morning.
Day 13	Day 14
Morning 1. Creatively combine any of the energy	Morning 1. Show gratitude for the good things in my life.

boosting foods listed in chapter one. 2. Call my mentor and find out how they are doing. Afternoon 1. Go for a 10-minute break and refresh the mind either with a chapter from a book or a short inspirational clip. Evening 1. Make a to-do list for the next day. 2. Make a list of things to be thankful for. 3. Take stock of any progress made during the day.	2. Make a short assessment of my major life goals and see how far I have come towards achieving them. 3. Produce a clearly defined strategy for the day ahead. Afternoon 1. Stay conscious and try to identify the major causes of my laziness. 2. Go through chapter eight of this book and remind yourself of its contents. Evening 1. Make a to-do list for the next day. 2. Make a list of things to be thankful for. 3. Take stock of any progress made during the day.
Day 15	Day 16
Morning 1. Listen to a motivating podcast. 2. Halfway through the 30-day plan: Assess myself and find out how well I have fared. Afternoon 1. Start an important task and timeframe for this task to be completed. 2. Take a short power nap. Evening	Morning 1. Get the mind to work by engaging in some mind games. 2. Clear work desk at work. 3. Break down all large projects into smaller ones. Afternoon 1. Take a short power nap. 2. Eat brain fruits like blueberries. 3. Spend one hour completing a major task. Evening

1. Go out and spend the night with a friend or colleague.	1. Evaluate and find out how much I have covered towards achieving my goals.
Day 17	**Day 18**
Morning 1. Creatively combine any of the energy boosting foods listed in chapter one. 2. No screen time until 9 AM. Use the time to finish up a major task. Afternoon 1. Go through chapter seven of this book and remind yourself of its contents. 2. Take a short power nap. 3. Eat brain fruits like blueberries. Evening 1. Go out and have fun. 2. Appreciate myself for any success recorded.	Morning 1. Creatively combine any of the energy boosting foods listed in chapter one. 2. Complete the hardest tasks of the day this morning. Afternoon 1. Try to find ways and reasons to love my job even better. 2. Break major tasks into bits. 3. Set a timeframe to complete each bit of broken-down tasks. 4. Do away with anything that may present itself as some sort of escape route from the task at hand. Evening 1. Make a short assessment of my major life goals and see how far I have come towards achieving them.
Day 19	**Day 20**
Morning 1. Go through chapter two of this book and remind yourself of its contents. 2. Creatively combine any of the energy	Morning 1. Listen to a motivating podcast. 2. Creatively combine any of the energy boosting foods listed in chapter one. Afternoon

boosting foods listed in chapter one. Afternoon 1. Break major tasks into bits. 2. Set a timeframe to complete each bit of broken-down tasks. 3. Do away with anything that may present itself as some sort of escape route from the task at hand. Evening 1. Talk to myself and address any form of fear of failure lingering in my mind. 2. Reaffirm some of the quotes listed in chapter three of this book.	1. Browse the internet and the study the lives of one successful person I admire. Evening 1. Make a list of major changes in my life since the beginning of the 30-day plan. 2. Reward myself.
Day 21	Day 22
Morning 1. Creatively combine any of the energy boosting foods listed in chapter one. 2. Start up a major task. Afternoon 1. No screen time until 3 PM. 2. Continue with the major task from the morning. Evening 1. Go out and reward yourself.	Morning 1. Listen to a motivating podcast. 2. Meditate Afternoon 1. Take a short power nap. 2. Eat brain fruits like blueberries. 3. Spend one hour completing a major task. Evening 1. Make a short assessment of my major life goals and

Stop Procrastination

	see how far I have come towards achieving them.
Day 23	Day 24
Morning 1. Get the mind to work by engaging in some mind games. Afternoon 1. Try to find ways and reasons to love my job even better. 2. Break major tasks into bits. 3. Set a timeframe to complete each bit of broken-down tasks. 4. Do away with anything that may present itself as some sort of escape route from the task at hand.	Morning 1. Listen to a motivating podcast. 2. Exercise for 10 minutes. Afternoon 1. Take a short power nap. 2. Eat brain fruits like blueberries. 3. Spend one hour completing a major task. Evening 1. Go out for a night with a colleague or friend.
Day 25	Day 26
Morning 1. No screen time till 9 AM. 2. Start on a major task. Afternoon 1. Study the task at hand and try to identify the benefits open to me if I am able to complete the specific task. 2. Have a short power nap. 3. Read a book and refresh the mind.	Morning 1. Creatively combine any of the energy boosting foods listed in chapter one. Afternoon 1. Study the task at hand and try to identify the benefits open to me if I am able to complete the specific task. 2. Have a short power nap. 3. Read a book and refresh the mind. Evening

Evening 1. Go through chapter six of this book and remind yourself of its contents. 2. Complete a major task.	1. Make a short assessment of my major life goals and see how far I have come towards achieving them.
Day 27	Day 28
Morning 1. Creatively combine any of the energy boosting foods listed in chapter one. 2. Assess my long-term plan and find out those that are not producing results. 3. Brainstorm new ideas and plan to create a better solution. Afternoon 1. No screen time until I complete a major task. 2. Task a short power nap. 3. Go for a walk and refresh my mind. 4. Carry out exercise four and the focus exercises listed in chapter five. Evening 1. Reward yourself for the day. 2. Assess yourself and find out how successful you have	Morning 1. Meditate for 10 minutes. 4. Go through chapter eight of this book and remind yourself of its contents. Afternoon 1. Study the task at hand and try to identify the benefits open to me if I am able to complete the specific task. 2. Have a short power nap. 3. Read a book and refresh the mind. Evening 1. Make a short assessment of my major life goals and see how far I have come towards achieving them.

Stop Procrastination

been throughout the week.	
Day 29	Day 30
Morning 1. Creatively combine any of the energy boosting foods listed in chapter one. Afternoon 1. Go through chapter three of this book and remind yourself of its contents. 2. Complete a major task before having any screen time. Evening 1. Call my mentor and ask for advice on some specific points of concern. 2. Make plans on how to implement the advice given.	Morning 1. Get the mind to work by engaging in some mind games. 2. Creatively combine any of the energy boosting foods listed in chapter one. Afternoon 1. Study the task at hand and try to identify the benefits open to me if I am able to complete the specific task. 2. Have a short power nap. 3. Read a book and refresh the mind. Evening 1. Make a short assessment of my major life goals and see how far I have come with achieving them. 2. Make assessments and see how far you have come in the 30-day plan.

Conclusion

It has indeed been a journey, and I believe that you have been motivated to get over procrastination and fire up your productivity. But remember, doesn't end there. You have to put in your efforts to achieve success finally. It is one thing to read an excellent book and be motivated, and it is another thing to put into practice everything that has been taught. It is action that differentiates a winner from a loser. So, which will it be for yours? Will you finish this book and forget everything that was taught? I hope not, because that would be a disaster. Begin to apply all of the tactics and techniques that have been listed and see your life change for the better.

I have simplified the instructions contained in this book for you, in the form of a 30-day plan. Follow the instructions given day after day, and follow it consistently and religiously. Remember that change is a gradual process. You might not notice the change on the first day, but with time you will see that you are no longer the same person. Research has proven that any action carried out consistently for more than 21 days finally becomes a habit. So, to create the habit of productivity, you have to follow the laid-out steps I have provided you. At the end of the 30 days, you will notice a great change in your life and have a testimony share with your friends.

I wish you success and more productivity in your life as you take action today. Remember, your mind is under your control.